MICROWAVE FOR ONE

MICROWAVE FOR ONE

Sonia Allison

Partridge Press

Acknowledgements

Loan of microwave, Electrolux

Loan of tableware, Le Pot, King Edwards Court, Windsor

Text copyright © 1987 by Sonia Allison

Photographs by Sue Atkinson

Designed by Victor Shreeve

Home Economist: Elaine Andrews

Published in Great Britain by

Partridge Press
Mawelton House
Haywards Heath
West Sussex

(Partridge Press is an imprint of
Transworld Publishers Ltd, 61-63 Uxbridge Road,
London W5 5SA)

Typeset by Clifford-Cooper Limited
The Mews, Farnham, Surrey

Printed and Bound in Great Britain by
Adlard & Son Ltd. The Garden City Press, Letchworth.

ISBN 1-85225-043-7

CONTENTS

Introduction

When I wrote my first microwave book in 1978, owners of domestic microwave ovens were few and far between and those who bought them were gambling on a new and experimental appliance, not too sure of themselves and wondering whether they had made a wise decision. Almost a decade later and the industry is booming as never before. The microwave has taken off like a rocket and become as much part and parcel of the kitchen scene as the toaster, kettle and washing machine, much appreciated by a rapidly growing number of users who find it not only invaluable for defrosting frozen foods in a hurry, but also for reheating home-cooked and shop-bought freezer meals, warming up soups and drinks, melting chocolate and fats, 'baking' jacket potatoes, scrambling eggs to perfection and cooking a surprisingly varied selection of sweet and savoury dishes which, before the technological age, needed a conventional oven and hob for success.

Additionally, the microwave has other distinct advantages. It is hygienic in use, simple to operate, remains cool to the touch, can be plugged in anywhere, keeps energy costs down, preserves nutrients in food and, treated knowingly, does a speedy and efficient job with unfailing reliability. It has built up a fan club of admirers from every age group and walk of life and, best of all, is *the* ideal appliance for those who cook solo, regularly or occasionally, and want to prepare a single serving snack or meal with minimum effort.

Looking back, I am sorry I was unable to put this book together earlier and come to the rescue of the many correspondents asking for microwave recipes for one; like college students sharing rented accommodation, the elderly living alone, working parents, busy professionals, factory workers and medical teams on shifts, cabin crews on airlines, teenagers. Hopefully, I cam make amends with this latest book and at the same time offer grateful thanks to all of you out there who took the trouble to write, telling me the sort of recipes you thought should be included. I have incorporated as many of your comments as I could and this newest collection is aimed specifically at cooks going it alone out of choice or necessity.

Practicality, as with all my books, has been a key consideration but occasionally a hint of luxury has slipped in when personal pampering seems justified. That apart, I have made sure the recipes are quick and easy to prepare, tending towards economy and not too demanding of obscure ingredients. Who, when cooking for themselves, wants a long list of items which they have to go out and buy, use twice and perhaps never touch again?

Dishes with fish, chicken, mince, eggs, cheese, vegetables and fruit are in plentiful supply because the microwave's track record for cooking these foods is impeccable. Likewise the pastas and rice, the lightest of light steamed puddings, even an individual Christmas one, stewed fruits and other desserts based on chocolate, jelly and custard. I have back-tracked on meat to some extent because it is very expensive, often toughens up in the microwave unless it is a prime cut and reacts better to conventional methods of cooking such as roasting, grilling, frying and stewing.

As you probably know, microwaved food left to its own devices comes out of the oven the same colour it went in — often pale and in need of brightening up. This is easy to achieve for savoury dishes by using stock granules, paprika, deep-toned cheeses, brown ketchups, Worcestershire and soy sauces, tomato ketchup or purée and adding toppings of crushed breakfast cereals or potato crisps, chopped nuts (toasted first), toasted breadcrumbs, appropriate herbs. Sweet dishes can be darkened with brown flours and sugar, spices such as cinnamon, jam, marmalade, honey and treacle. All are basically natural additives to achieve the desired colour effect.

Dishes throughout the book have been tested in a 600 watt oven at either full power or defrost settings. Times for microwaves of different wattage have been calculated for you, appearing in a table at the end of each recipe. Another factor: as people work at different rates, from the pace of a snail to a streak of lightning, I have *not* given preparation times but described instead whether a dish is demanding, fiddly, child's play, attention-seeking and so on. You will find the description directly under the recipe title and should give you some idea of what you are letting yourself in for.

A few reminders
1. Unless otherwise specified, the microwave should be fitted with a 13 amp plug.
2. A microwave works by agitating liquid (usually water) contained in food. This in turn vibrates at a vigorous rate to create high heat; rather like rubbing ones hands together briskly on a cold day for warmth.
3. To prevent damage, the oven should *never* be switched on when empty.
4. Metal cooking containers, or dishes with metal trims, are unsuitable for use in the microwave. Recommended are glass (but *not* crystal), pottery, all types of specially designed microwave cookware, roasting or boiling polythene bags tied with rubber bands or string, and rigid plastic. Please note that certain kinds of dark dishes become very hot and uncomfortable to handle without oven gloves.
5. Although microwaved utensils are supposed to stay fairly cool to the touch, they frequently absorb heat from the hot food inside and, like dark dishes, should be removed from the oven with hands protected by oven gloves or a teatowel.
6. For covering, use matching lids, kitchen paper or cling wrap, making sure it is the newer kind *without* plasticisers. Also check manufacturer's pack instructions as some makes of wrap *must not* be punctured.
7. Standing times, following on from cooking, encourage heat to travel from the edges of the food to the centre. This does away with lengthier cooking times which might otherwise toughen the food beyond repair and/or cause unappetising dryness.
8. Microwaves cook very rapidly indeed. Therefore avoid adding on an extra few seconds or so 'for good measure' as the dish might turn out to be a complete disaster.
9. Do not try to double up recipes if you are entertaining. It rarely works successfully and it is safer to cook the same dish twice or three times. Moreover, do not take, say, a recipe from another micorwave book geared for four and try to adapt it to a one-serving portion as the likelihood of it working well is remote. Finally, *never* try to adapt conventional recipes to microwave cooking.

Sonia Allison,
Hertfordshire,
1987

BITS
AND PIECES

All recipes have been tested in a 600 watt oven.
See chart under each for variations of wattage.

PUPPADOMS (Poppadums)

Preparation — a doddle

Packets of puppadoms keep almost indefinitely and are therefore an excellent investment for curry lovers. When you next bring home a take-away Indian meal, why not prepare your own puppadoms in the microwave?

2 x 5 inch (12.5 cm) puppadoms

1. Put puppadoms on to a plate, one on top of the other.
2. Leave uncovered.
3. Cook at full power for 2½ minutes, turning both over at half time.
4. Serve while still hot.

Watts	Full Power	Defrost
400	3 mins 20 secs	Nil
500	2 mins 55 secs	Nil
600	2 mins 30 secs	Nil
650	2 mins 20 secs	Nil
700	2 mins 5 secs	Nil

BAKED BEANS ON TOAST

Preparation — effortless

The universal snack meal of Great Britain, now simply heated in the microwave on top of a slice of toast. Because beans pop if heated too quickly, I have opted for defrost setting.

> **1 large slice freshly made toast**
> **1 can (5 oz or 150 g) baked beans**

1. Place toast on serving plate.
2. Top with beans. Leave uncovered.
3. Warm through at defrost setting for 3½ minutes. Serve.

Watts	Full Power	Defrost
400	Nil	4 min 40 secs
500	Nil	4 min 5 secs
600	Nil	3 min 30 secs
650	Nil	3 min 15 secs
700	Nil	2 min 55 secs

SPAGHETTI ON TOAST

Preparation — effortless

Make as above, covering toast with 1 can (7½ oz or 213 g) spaghetti in tomato sauce. Cook as below.

Watts	Full Power	Defrost
400	3 mins 20 secs	Nil
500	2 mins 55 secs	Nil
600	2 mins 30 secs	Nil
650	2 mins 20 secs	Nil
700	2 mins 5 secs	Nil

CALIFORNIAN TOFU SALAD

Preparation — a little bit demanding

High protein, low calorie tofu (available from health food shops) is an inexpensive product made from soya beans. It looks like firm cream cheese and readily absorbs flavours of other foods. This salad is a substantial meal on its own and all it needs is some crisp bread or rolls to add contrast of texture.

2 medium tomatoes
3 spring onions
5 oz (150 g) tofu (half a packet)
6 teaspoons salad oil
3 teaspoons lemon juice
½ level teaspoon garlic salt
¼ level teaspoon plain salt
½ level teaspoon caster sugar
8 black or green olives or use capers if preferred

1. Wash and dry tomatoes. Cut into small cubes. Trim spring onions. Coarsely chop. Leave aside for the moment.
2. Cut tofu into ½ inch (1.25 cm) cubes. Put into dish. Stir in all remaining ingredients except olives or capers.
3. Cover with a saucer. Heat at defrost setting for 3 minutes.
4. Uncover. Mix in tomatoes and onions. Re-cover as above.
5. Leave until cold. Refrigerate 2 hours. Garnish with olives or capers. Serve.

Watts	Full Power	Defrost
400	Nil	4 mins
500	Nil	3 min 30 secs
600	Nil	3 mins
650	Nil	2 min 45 secs
700	Nil	2 min 30 secs

CHILI MADE WITH TOFU

Preparation — easy

Based on economically-priced tofu (soya bean curd which is bland, firm, creamy-colour, protein-packed and low in calories), this is a super chili for non-meat eaters and goes beautifully with rice or shop-bought and reheated Mexican-style tortillas.

5 oz (150 g) tofu (half a packet)

1 can (5 oz or 150 g) baked beans in tomato sauce

½ level teaspoon mild chili seasoning (or powder)

1 level tablespoon tomato purée

2 tablespoons water

1 peeled and crushed garlic clove or ½ inch (1.25 cm) tubed garlic purée

¼ level teaspoon salt

1. Cut tofu into ½ inch (1.25 cm) cubes.
2. Put into 1 pint (575 ml) serving dish.
3. Stir in rest of ingredients.
4. Cover with a plate or saucer. Leave to stand for 1 hour so that tofu absorbs flavours from its companions.
5. Cover with cling wrap. Puncture twice with the tip of a knife to prevent a build-up of steam underneath. (See page 8.)
6. Cook at full power for 4 minutes. Uncover. Stir round and serve.

Watts	Full Power	Defrost
400	5 mins 20 secs	Nil
500	4 mins 40 secs	Nil
600	4 mins	Nil
650	3 mins 40 secs	Nil
700	3 mins 20 secs	Nil

THE CROISSANTERIE

Preparation — all easy

Come into the *croissanterie chez moi* and enjoy a selection of the trendiest sandwiches in the business — delicately warm croissants with an assortment of fillings. Each will make a most generous lunch or supper snack and teams perfectly with hot coffee, foamy chocolate or tea.

CHEESE AND CRESS CROISSANT

> **1 straight croissant, 6 or 7 inches (15 to 18 cm) in length**
> **1 oz (25 g) cream cheese (St. Ivel lactic is an interesting choice)**
> **¼ box mustard and cress, well washed**

1. Split croissant.
2. Spread both sides with cheese. Sandwich together with cress.
3. Put on to plate. Leave uncovered.
4. Heat at defrost setting for 20 to 25 seconds or until croissant feels warm. Serve.

Watts	Full Power	Defrost
400	Nil	26 to 33 secs
500	Nil	23 to 29 secs
600	Nil	20 to 25 secs
650	Nil	18 to 23 secs
700	Nil	17 to 21 secs

THE BLT

This is a North American special and the initials stand for bacon, lettuce and tomato. It's a vast sandwich, match-made for icy beer and a healthy appetite.

> **1 round croissant, about 4 inches (10 cm) across**
> **butter or margarine**
> **2 oz (50 g) back bacon**
> **3 oz (75 g) tomato, washed and sliced**
> **2 soft lettuce leaves**

1. Split croissant. Spread with butter or margarine.
2. Put bacon on plate. Cover loosely with kitchen paper towels. Cook at defrost setting for 2 minutes.
3. Sandwich croissant together with warm bacon, tomato and lettuce.
4. Put on to plate. Leave uncovered.
5. Heat at defrost setting for 40 to 50 seconds or until croissant feels warm. Serve.

Watts	Full Power	Defrost
400	Nil	2 mins 40 secs; 52 secs to 1 min 5 secs
500	Nil	2 mins 20 secs; 46 secs to 1 min
600	Nil	2 mins; 40 to 50 secs
650	Nil	1 min 50 secs; 37 to 45 secs
700	Nil	1 min 40 secs; 34 to 40 secs

BEARNAISE CROISSANT WITH HAM AND CUCUMBER

1 straight croissant, 6 or 7 inches (15 to 18 cm) in length
3 rounded teaspoons Bearnaise sauce (bottled)
2 oz (50 g) ham
6 thin slices of unpeeled cucumber

1. Split croissant.
2. Spread both sides with Bearnaise sauce.
3. Sandwich together with ham and cucumber.
4. Put on to plate. Leave uncovered.
5. Heat at defrost setting for 40 to 45 seconds or until croissant feels warm. Serve.

Watts	Full Power	Defrost
400	Nil	52 secs to 1 min
500	Nil	46 to 55 secs
600	Nil	40 to 45 secs
650	Nil	37 to 40 secs
700	Nil	34 to 36 secs

BLOATER AND BEET CROISSANT

1 straight croissant, 6 or 7 inches (15 to 18 cm) in length
1 jar (just over the ounce or 35 g) bloater paste
5 sprigs watercress
1 oz (25g) sliced pickled beetroot

1. Split croissant.
2. Spread both sides with bloater paste.
3. Sandwich together with watercress and the beetroot.
4. Put on to plate. Leave uncovered.
5. Heat at defrost setting for 25 to 30 seconds or until croissant feels warm. Serve.

Watts	Full Power	Defrost
400	Nil	33 to 40 secs
500	Nil	29 to 35 secs
600	Nil	25 to 30 secs
650	Nil	23 to 28 secs
700	Nil	21 to 25 secs

CAMEMBERT AND PICKLED CUCUMBER CROISSANT

1 straight croissant, 6 or 7 inches (15 to 18 cm) in length
2 oz (50 g) soft, but not runny, Camembert cheese (weighed without rind)
1 oz (25 g) pickled cucumber, thinly sliced

1. Split croissant.
2. Spread with cheese. Sandwich together with cucumber.
3. Put on to plate. Leave uncovered.
4. Heat at defrost setting for 25 to 30 seconds or until croissant feels warm. Serve.

Watts	Full Power	Defrost
400	Nil	33 to 40 secs
500	Nil	29 to 35 secs
600	Nil	25 to 30 secs
650	Nil	23 to 28 secs
700	Nil	21 to 25 secs

PÂTÉ AND LETTUCE CROISSANT

> 1 round croissant, about 4 inches (10 cm) across
> 2 oz (50 g) liver pâté
> 2 soft lettuce leaves

1. Split croissant.
2. Spread both sides with pâté.
3. Sandwich together with lettuce.
4. Put on to plate. Leave uncovered.
5. Heat at defrost setting for 25 to 30 seconds or until croissant feels warm. Serve.

Watts	Full Power	Defrost
400	Nil	33 to 40 secs
500	Nil	29 to 35 secs
600	Nil	25 to 30 secs
650	Nil	23 to 28 secs
700	Nil	21 to 25 secs

BEEF AND HORSERADISH CROISSANT WITH PICKLE

> 1 round croissant, about 4 inches (10 cm) across
> butter or margarine
> ½ jar (about 1 oz or 25 g) beef pâté
> 2 level teaspoons creamed horseradish
> 1 level tablespoon pickled red cabbage, well drained

1. Split croissant.
2. Spread with butter or margarine followed by pâté and horseradish.
3. Sandwich together with red cabbage.
4. Put on to plate. Leave uncovered.
5. Heat at defrost setting for 25 to 30 seconds or until croissant feels warm. Serve.

Watts	Full Power	Defrost
400	Nil	33 to 40 secs
500	Nil	29 to 35 secs
600	Nil	25 to 30 secs
650	Nil	23 to 28 secs
700	Nil	21 to 25 secs

SALMON AND SHRIMP CROISSANT WITH RADICCHIO

1 round croissant, about 4 inches (10 cm) across
1 jar (just over 1 oz or 35 g) salmon and shrimp paste
4 leaves radicchio

1. Split croissant.
2. Spread with paste.
3. Sandwich together with radicchio.
4. Put on to plate. Leave uncovered.
5. Heat at defrost setting for 25 to 30 seconds or until croissant feels warm. Serve.

Watts	Full Power	Defrost
400	Nil	33 to 40 secs
500	Nil	29 to 35 secs
600	Nil	25 to 30 secs
650	Nil	23 to 28 secs
700	Nil	21 to 25 secs

PEANUT BUTTER AND MARMITE

1 round croissant, about 4 inches (10 cm) across
2 level teaspoons chunky peanut butter
Marmite or Vecon

1. Split croissant.
2. Spread with peanut butter and Marmite or Vecon.
3. Put on to plate. Leave uncovered.
4. Heat at defrost setting for 25 to 30 seconds or until croissant feels warm. Serve.

Watts	Full Power	Defrost
400	Nil	33 to 40 secs
500	Nil	29 to 35 secs
600	Nil	25 to 30 secs
650	Nil	23 to 28 secs
700	Nil	21 to 25 secs

COTTAGE CHEESE AND JAM CROISSANT

> 1 round croissant, about 4 inches (10 cm) across
>
> 2 rounded tablespoons cottage cheese
>
> 2 level teaspoons jam, flavour to taste

1. Split croissant.
2. Spread with cottage cheese.
3. Dot with jam. Sandwich together.
4. Put on to plate. Leave uncovered.
5. Heat at defrost setting for 25 to 30 seconds or until croissant feels warm. Serve.

Watts	Full Power	Defrost
400	Nil	33 to 40 secs
500	Nil	29 to 35 secs
600	Nil	25 to 30 secs
650	Nil	23 to 28 secs
700	Nil	21 to 25 secs

BANANA AND LEMON CURD CROISSANT

> 1 round croissant, about 4 inches (10 cm) across
>
> 2 level tablespoons lemon curd
>
> ½ medium banana, peeled and sliced

1. Split croissant.
2. Spread with lemon curd.
3. Sandwich together with banana.
4. Put on to plate. Leave uncovered.
5. Heat at defrost setting for 25 to 30 seconds or until croissant feels warm. Serve.

Watts	Full Power	Defrost
400	Nil	33 to 40 secs
500	Nil	29 to 35 secs
600	Nil	25 to 30 secs
650	Nil	23 to 28 secs
700	Nil	21 to 25 secs

TUMBLING CRANBERRY NOG

Preparation — fairly speedy

If you want the lightest of dreams to go to bed with, this nog is the perfect answer.

> **2 rounded tablespoons bottled cranberry sauce**
> **1 Grade 2 egg**
> **pinch of salt**

1. Put cranberry sauce into a ½ pint (275 ml) non-crystal tumbler.
2. Separate egg, adding yolk to cranberry sauce and dropping white into a clean, dry bowl.
3. Stir yolk into sauce until smooth.
4. Beat egg white and salt to a stiff snow.
5. Fold gently into sauce and yolk mixture.
6. Heat at full power for ½ minute. Eat straightaway with a spoon.

TIP
Raspberry or plum jam may be used instead of the cranberry sauce.

Watts	Full Power	Defrost
400	40 secs	Nil
500	35 secs	Nil
600	30 secs	Nil
650	28 secs	Nil
700	25 secs	Nil

HOT CHOCOLATE SAUCE

Preparation — quite unproblematic

A perfect sauce for chocoholics and designed for spooning over ice cream and ice cream sundaes.

> **1 tablespoon milk**
> **1 level tablespoon dark brown soft sugar**
> **1 level teaspoon drinking chocolate**
> **1 oz (25 g) plain chocolate, broken into cubes**

1. Put milk and sugar into a small dish. Leave uncovered.
2. Heat at defrost setting for 1 minute.
3. Add remaining ingredients. Leave uncovered.
4. Heat at defrost setting for a further minute.
5. Stir briskly until completely smooth. Use warm.

Watts	Full Power	Defrost
400	Nil	1 min 20 secs; 1 min 20 secs
500	Nil	1 min 10 secs; 1 min 10 secs
600	Nil	1 min; 1 min
650	Nil	55 secs; 55 secs
700	Nil	50 secs; 50 secs

MOCHA SAUCE

Preparation — a doddle

Splendidly easy, this makes an exceptional warm topping for ice cream and sorbet — too hard to resist!

1 oz (25 g) plain chocolate
2 teaspoons liquid coffee essence
1 teaspoon milk or cream

1. Break chocolate into a small dish or cup.
2. Add coffee essence and milk or cream.
3. Leave uncovered. Heat at defrost setting for 1½ minutes.
4. Stir briskly until smooth. Use warm.

Watts	Full Power	Defrost
400	Nil	2 mins
500	Nil	1 min 45 secs
600	Nil	1 min 30 secs
650	Nil	1 min 25 secs
700	Nil	1 min 15 secs

SERENDIPITY SOUP

Preparation — a little time-consuming

A warming, colourful blend which converts into the most comforting and economical winter soup. Filling, too.

1 level teaspoon cornflour
¼ level teaspoon mild chili seasoning
½ level teaspoon stock or gravy granules
¼ pt (150 ml) water
1 level tablespoon mixed dried peppers
1 can (about 7 oz or 213 g) red kidney beans and liquor
¼ level teaspoon garlic salt
4 oz (125 g) pork or beef sausages, each cut into 5 chunks
2 level teaspoons tomato purée

1. Mix cornflour, chili seasoning and stock or gravy granules smoothly with water.
2. Pour into a 1 pint (575 ml) round dish. Stir in peppers and beans with the thick liquor from can.
3. Cover with cling wrap. Puncture twice with the tip of a knife to prevent a build-up of steam underneath. (See page 8.) Alternatively, use matching lid.
4. Cook at full power for 4 minutes.
5. Uncover. Stir in garlic salt, sausages and purée.
6. Re-cover. Cook at full power for 3 minutes.
7. Stand 2 minutes. Uncover, stir round and serve.

Watts	Full Power	Defrost
400	5 mins 20 secs; 4 mins	Nil
500	4 mins 40 secs; 3 mins 30 secs	Nil
600	4 mins; 3 mins	Nil
650	3 mins 40 secs; 2 mins 45 secs	Nil
700	3 mins 20 secs; 2 mins 30 secs	Nil

FISH

All recipes have been tested in a 600 watt oven.
See chart under each for variations of wattage.

FISH DISHES

1. Fish used has been taken from the refrigerator and allowed to 'warm up' for about seven to ten minutes.
2. When fish has been used from frozen, this is clearly indicated in the recipe.

TUNA TOPPED MAYONNAISE TOAST

Preparation — reasonably fast

A delicious combination, perfect for lunch or supper with some coleslaw salad or cut-up tomatoes.

1 large slice white or brown toast
2 level tablespoons thick mayonnaise
1 can (3½ oz or 99 g) tuna in vegetable oil or brine
1 large slice processed cheese (about 1½ oz or 40 g)
paprika
watercress or parsley for garnish (optional)

1. Put toast on to a plate. Spread with mayonnaise.
2. Drain tuna. Flake up flesh and use to cover toast.
3. Break cheese into 4 pieces. Arrange over tuna.
4. Cook, uncovered, at defrost setting for 2 minutes.
5. Dust with paprika. Garnish to taste with watercress or parsley.

Watts	Full Power	Defrost
400	Nil	2 mins 40 secs
500	Nil	2 mins 20 secs
600	Nil	2 mins
650	Nil	1 mins 50 secs
700	Nil	1 mins 40 secs

BUTTERED TROUT IN PERNOD

Preparation — easy

Something to appeal to those who appreciate the taste of aniseed. Certainly it's unusual.

1 x 12 oz (350 g) trout, cleaned but with head left on
½ oz (15 g) butter or margarine
¼ level teaspoon salt
¼ level teaspoon paprika
2 tablespoons Pernod (or use Ricard if preferred)
parsley for garnishing

1. Wash and drain trout. Put on to a plate.
2. Place butter or margarine into a cup. Melt, uncovered at defrost setting for about 1 minute.
3. Add all remaining ingredients. Stir well. Pour over fish.
4. Cover with cling wrap. Puncture twice with the tip of a knife to prevent a build-up of steam underneath. (See page 8.)
5. Cook at full power for 4½ minutes.
6. Stand 1 minute. Uncover. Garnish with parsley. Serve.

Watts	Full Power	Defrost
400	5 mins 55 secs	1 min 20 secs
500	5 mins 15 secs	1 min 10 secs
600	4 mins 30 secs	1 min
650	4 mins 10 secs	55 secs
700	3 mins 45 secs	50 secs

FAR EAST SOLE

Preparation — requires a bit of effort

Anyone into Oriental-style food will enjoy sole cooked with Teriyaki sauce, ginger and garlic. It has a superb fragrance and flavour, predictably best with rice — white or brown — and mange tout or broccoli.

½ oz (15 g) fresh ginger, peeled and grated

1 garlic clove, peeled and crushed

1 tablespoon Teriyaki sauce

1 lemon sole (8 oz or 225 g), trimmed weight

spring onion for garnish (optional)

1.   Mix together ginger, garlic and Teriyaki sauce.
2.   Wash and drain sole. Put on to a large plate.
3.   Coat with Teriyaki mixture.
4.   Cover with cling wrap. Puncture twice with the tip of a knife to prevent a build-up of steam underneath. (See page 8.)
5.   Cook at full power for 3½ to 4 minutes when fish should look flaky and tender.
6.   Stand 1 minute. Uncover. Serve.

Watts	Full Power	Defrost
400	4 mins 40 secs to 5 mins 20 secs	Nil
500	4 mins 5 secs to 4 mins 40 secs	Nil
600	3 mins 30 secs to 4 mins	Nil
650	3 mins 15 secs to 3 mins 40 secs	Nil
700	2 mins 55 secs to 3 mins 20 secs	Nil

SOLE IN ROSE MARIE SAUCE

Preparation — fairly easy

Unusually cooked in a very up-and-coming cocktail sauce, the sole turns out to be a ritzy dish, quite at its best with new potatoes and a green salad based on friseé (which was once known as curly endive), cucumber, tomatoes and pepper strips.

2 level tablespoons tomato ketchup
2 rounded tablespoons thick mayonnaise (*not* salad cream)
1 teaspoon Worcestershire sauce
1 teaspoon medium or sweet sherry
a shake of Tabasco or cayenne pepper
1 lemon sole (8 oz or 225 g), trimmed weight
2 slices of lemon for garnish
parsley or watercress for garnish (optional)

1. Mix together ketchup, mayonnaise, Worcestershire sauce, sherry and Tabasco or cayenne pepper.
2. Wash and drain sole. Put on to a large plate.
3. Coat with mayonnaise mixture.
4. Cover with cling wrap. Puncture twice with the tip of a knife to prevent a build-up of steam underneath. (See page 8.))
5. Cook at full power for 3½ to 4 minutes when fish should look flaky and tender.
6. Stand 1 minute. Uncover. Garnish. Serve.

Watts	Full Power	Defrost
400	4 mins 40 secs to 5 mins 20 secs	Nil
500	4 mins 5 secs to 4 mins 40 secs	Nil
600	3 mins 30 secs to 4 mins	Nil
650	3 mins 15 secs to 3 mins 40 secs	Nil
700	2 mins 55 secs to 3 mins 20 secs	Nil

SOFT HERRING ROES IN GARLIC BUTTER

Preparation — reasonably fast

Very much in the haute cuisine class, the roes team fashionably with a warm croissant.

4 oz (125 g) soft herring roes, as fresh as possible
½ oz (15 g) butter or margarine
1 garlic clove, peeled and crushed
⅛ level teaspoon salt
pepper to taste
1 level teaspoon chopped fresh basil or fresh coriander

1. Wash roes, drain well and put into a fairly small but deepish cooking dish.
2. Cut butter or magarine into thin flakes. Arrange over roes.
3. Crush garlic and sprinkle on top, along with salt and pepper.
4. Cover with cling wrap. Puncture twice with the tip of a knife to prevent a build-up of steam underneath. (See page 8.) Alternatively, use matching lid.
5. Cook at defrost setting for 5 minutes.
6. Stand 1 minute. Uncover. Sprinkle with basil or coriander. Serve.

Watts	Full Power	Defrost
400	Nil	6 mins 40 secs
500	Nil	5 mins 50 secs
600	Nil	5 mins
650	Nil	4 mins 35 secs
700	Nil	4 mins 10 secs

SOFT HERRING ROES IN MILK SAUCE

Preparation — easy

A delight for those who enjoy soft roes. You can eat them straight from the dish with hot toast.

4 oz (125 g) soft herring roes, as fresh as possible

1 level teaspoon cornflour

4 tablespoons cold milk

¼ level teaspoon salt

pepper to taste

1. Wash roes, drain well and put into a fairly small but deepish cooking dish.
2. Blend cornflour smoothly with milk. Add salt and pepper to taste.
3. Pour over roes. Turn over and over gently to mix.
4. Cover with cling wrap, puncturing it twice with the tip of a knife prevent a build-up of steam underneath. (See page 8.) Alternatively, use matching lid.
5. Cook at defrost setting for 5½ minutes.
6. Stand 1 minute. Uncover. Serve.

Tip
If liked, sprinkle with fresh chopped parsley.

Watts	Full Power	Defrost
400	Nil	7 mins 15 secs
500	Nil	6 mins 25 secs
600	Nil	5 mins 30 secs
650	Nil	5 mins 5 secs
700	Nil	4 mins 35 secs

OLD-FASHIONED HERRING

Preparation — easy and straightforward

A dash of piquancy and herbs add style and flavour to this tasty herring dish.

> **1 fresh, medium herring, 4 to 5 oz (125 g to 150 g), weighed *after* cleaning and minus head**
> **1 tablespoon malt vinegar**
> **¼ level teaspoon mixed herbs**
> **½ level teaspoon onion salt**
> **pepper to taste**

1.   Wash herring and put on to a large plate, flesh side facing.
2.   Coat with malt vinegar.
3.   Sprinkle with herbs, salt and pepper to taste.
4.   Cover with cling wrap. Puncture twice with the tip of a knife to prevent a build-up of steam underneath. (See page 8.)
5.   Cook at full power for 1½ to 2 minutes or until fish starts making popping sounds and flesh looks flaky and tender.
6.   Stand 1 minute. Uncover. Serve.

Watts	Full Power	Defrost
400	2 mins 45 secs to 2 mins 40 secs	Nil
500	1 min 45 secs to 2 mins 20 secs	Nil
600	1 min 30 secs to 2 mins	Nil
650	1 min 25 secs to 1 min 50 secs	Nil
700	1 min 15 secs to 1 min 40 secs	Nil

HEREFORD HERRING

Preparation — easy and straightforward

A finely-flavoured herring dish which is ready in about two minutes and specially designed for slimmers. By way of accompaniment try a crisp salad, homemade or shop-bought.

> **1 fresh, medium herring, 4 to 5 oz (125 to 150 g), weighed** *after* **cleaning and minus head**
> **dried thyme**
> **⅛ level teaspoon salt**
> **pepper to taste**
> **1 tablespoon apple juice**

1. Wash herring and put on to a large plate, flesh side facing.
2. Sprinkle with thyme, salt and pepper to taste.
3. Pour apple juice round fish.
4. Cover with cling wrap. Puncture twice with the tip of a knife to prevent a build-up of steam underneath. (See page 8.)
5. Cook at full power for 1½ to 2 minutes or until fish starts making popping sounds and flesh looks flaky and tender.
6. Stand 1 minute. Uncover. Serve.

Watts	Full Power	Defrost
400	2 mins to 2 mins 40 secs	Nil
500	1 min 45 secs to 2 mins 20 secs	Nil
600	1 min 30 secs to 2 mins	Nil
650	1 min 25 secs to 1 min 50 secs	Nil
700	1 min 15 secs to 1 min 40 secs	Nil

TANDOORI HERRING

Preparation — easy and straightforward

Unusually-flavoured, here is a lively way of serving herring. Eat with rice or warm pitta bread.

> **1 fresh, medium herring, 4 to 5 oz (125 g to 150 g), weighed**
> **_after_ cleaning and minus head**
>
> **1 tablespoon fresh lemon juice**
>
> **salt**
>
> **1 level teaspoon Tandoori spice mix**

1. Wash herring and put on to a large plate, flesh side facing.
2. Coat with lemon juice.
3. Sprinkle with salt and spice mix.
4. Cover with cling wrap. Puncture twice with the tip of a knife to prevent a build-up of steam underneath. (See page 8.)
5. Cook at full power for 1½ to 2 minutes or until fish starts making popping sounds and flesh looks flaky and tender.
6. Stand 1 minute. Uncover. Serve.

Watts	Full Power	Defrost
400	2 mins 45 secs to 2 mins 40 secs	Nil
500	1 min 45 secs to 2 mins 20 secs	Nil
600	1 min 30 secs to 2 mins	Nil
650	1 min 25 secs to 1 min 50 secs	Nil
700	1 min 15 secs to 1 min 40 secs	Nil

Egg Mayonnaise/Croissants: Cheese and Cress; Salmon and Shrimp with Radicchio

Meat-Stuffed Pepper/Marinated Cauliflower

Far East Sole/Malay-Style Chicken

Curried Mince/Puppadoms

ITALIAN HERRING

Preparation — easy and straightforward

I made a note to myself which read 'divine' after tasting the herring. Try it and see for yourselves if you agree!

---

1 fresh, medium herring, 4 to 5 oz (125 g to 150 g), weighed *after* cleaning and minus head

1 tablespoon tomato juice

⅛ teaspoon salt

⅛ teaspoon dried basil

pepper to taste

---

1. Wash herring and put on to a large plate, flesh side facing.
2. Coat with tomato juice.
3. Sprinkle with salt, basil and pepper to taste.
4. Cover with cling wrap. Puncture twice with the tip of a knife to prevent a build-up of steam underneath. (See page 8.)
5. Cook at full power for 1½ to 2 minutes or until fish starts making popping sounds and flesh looks flaky and tender.
6. Stand 1 minute. Uncover. Serve.

Watts	Full Power	Defrost
400	2 mins 45 secs to 2 mins 40 secs	Nil
500	1 min 45 secs to 2 mins 20 secs	Nil
600	1 min 30 secs to 2 mins	Nil
650	1 min 25 secs to 1 min 50 secs	Nil
700	1 min 15 secs to 1 min 40 secs	Nil

MACKEREL IN APPLE SAUCE

Preparation — a doddle

A pleasing mackerel dish which responds well to the addition of apple sauce.

1 fresh mackerel, 7 oz (200 g), weighed *after* cleaning and minus head
⅛ teaspoon salt
pepper to taste
1 baby can (128 g) apple sauce or use same weight from a larger jar
wedge of lemon

1. Wash mackerel and put on to a large plate, flesh side facing.
2. Sprinkle with salt and pepper.
3. Coat with apple sauce.
4. Cover with cling wrap. Puncture twice with the tip of a knife to prevent a build-up of steam underneath. (See page 8.)
5. Cook at full power for 3½ minutes or until fish starts to make popping sounds.
6. Stand 1 minute. Uncover. Add lemon. Serve.

Watts	Full Power	Defrost
400	4 mins 40 secs	Nil
500	4 mins 5 secs	Nil
600	3 mins 30 secs	Nil
650	3 mins 15 secs	Nil
700	2 mins 55 secs	Nil

CLASSIC POACHED SALMON

Preparation — fast

With fresh and frozen salmon more in evidence than ever before, why not treat yourself to a cutlet or steak for Sunday lunch? This is a simple poached version eaten hot with butter but, if the amount seems to be daunting and too much for one go, eat half hot and keep the rest for a cold salmon mayonnaise. Two meals for the price of one and no cooking the second time around!

1 salmon steak or cutlet (about 8 to 9 oz or 225 to 250 g), thawed completely if frozen
1 tablespoon lemon juice
2 tablespoons white wine or water
1 small bay leaf
1 sprig of parsley
¼ level teaspoon salt
lemon to accompany

1. Wash and dry salmon and put into a 1 pint (575 ml) round cooking dish.
2. Add lemon juice, wine or water, bay leaf and parsley. Sprinkle with salt.
3. Cover with cling wrap. Puncture twice with the tip of a knife to prevent a build-up of steam underneath. (See page 8.) Alternatively, use matching lid.
4. Cook at full power for 3 minutes.
5. Stand 2 minutes, uncover, transfer to a plate and top with butter or margarine. Accompany with a wedge of lemon.

Watts	Full Power	Defrost
400	4 mins	Nil
500	3 mins 30 secs	Nil
600	3 mins	Nil
650	2 mins 45 secs	Nil
700	2 mins 30 secs	Nil

POACHED SALMON IN MANDARIN BUTTER

Preparation — easy

A sophisticated and stylish way of preparing salmon. It is in total harmony with small new potatoes, slender French beans and button mushrooms.

1 salmon steak or cutlet (about 8 to 9 oz or 225 to 250 g), thawed completely if frozen
½ oz (15 oz) butter or margarine
finely grated peel of ½ a mandarin or clementine
¼ level teaspoon salt
watercress to garnish

1. Wash and dry salmon. Transfer to a large plate.
2. Put butter or margarine in a cup. Melt, uncovered, at defrost setting for about 1 minute.
3. Stir in fruit peel.
4. Spoon over salmon. Sprinkle with salt.
5. Cover with cling wrap. Puncture twice with the tip of a knife to prevent a build-up of steam underneath. (See page 8.)
6. Cook at full power for 3 minutes.
7. Stand 2 minutes. Uncover. Garnish with watercress. Serve.

Watts	Full Power	Defrost
400	4 mins	1 min 20 secs
500	3 mins 30 secs	1 min 10 secs
600	3 mins	1 min
650	2 mins 45 secs	55 secs
700	2 mins 30 secs	50 secs

POACHED SALMON IN MUSTARD SAUCE

Preparation — easy

Elegant and sophisticated for special occasions, the blend of ingredients creates its own French-style sauce, seasoning the fish to perfection. Serve with very thinly sliced cucumber, slightly salted and tossed with salad dressing. Also French bread and butter or crusty rolls.

1 salmon steak or cutlet (about 8 to 9 oz or 225 to 250 g), thawed completely if frozen
½ oz (15 g) butter or margarine
1 level teaspoon Dijon mustard
¼ level teaspoon salt
2 teaspoons vinegar

1. Wash and dry salmon. Transfer to a large plate.
2. Put butter or margarine into a cup. Melt, uncovered, at defrost setting for about 1 minute.
3. Mix in rest of ingredients.
4. Spoon over salmon.
5. Cover with cling wrap. Puncture twice with the tip of a knife to prevent a build-up of steam underneath. (See page 8.)
6. Cook at full power for 3 minutes.
7. Stand 2 minutes. Uncover. Serve.

Watts	Full Power	Defrost
400	4 mins	1 min 20 secs
500	3 mins 30 secs	1 min 10 secs
600	3 mins	1 min
650	2 mins 45 secs	55 secs
700	2 mins 30 secs	50 secs

SAGE AND ONION HADDOCK OR HAKE

Preparation — easy

In no way run-of-the-mill, this makes a hearty and flavourful main course with vegetables to taste.

1 hake or haddock cutlet, weighing about 8 oz or 225 g
½ oz (15 g) butter or margarine
2 tablespoons milk
2 level tablespoons sage and onion stuffing mix, used dry
1 rounded tablespoon chopped parsley

1. Wash and dry cutlet. Transfer to a large plate.
2. Put butter or margarine into a cup. Melt, uncovered, at defrost setting for about 1 minute.
3. Stir in milk. Pour gently around fish.
4. Sprinkle stuffing mix over fish.
5. Cover with cling wrap. Puncture twice with the tip of a knife to prevent a build-up of steam underneath. (See page 8.)
6. Cook at full power for 4 minutes.
7. Stand 1 minute. Uncover. Sprinkle with parsley. Serve.

Watts	Full Power	Defrost
400	5 mins 20 secs	1 min 20 secs
500	4 mins 40 secs	1 min 10 secs
600	4 mins	1 min
650	3 mins 40 secs	55 secs
700	3 mins 20 secs	50 secs

LUXURY HADDOCK OR HAKE WITH CRAB

Preparation — requires a bit of effort

Out-of-the-ordinary and expensive-tasting, this can give you haute cuisine in minutes and its recommended partners are rice or potatoes and a tossed green salad. Or broccoli.

1 hake or haddock cutlet, weighing about 8 oz or 225 g
1 can (43 g or about 1½ oz) dressed crab
1 slightly rounded tablespoon mayonnaise
2 teaspoons lemon juice
2 spring onions
⅛ level teaspoon paprika
lemon for garnishing

1. Wash and dry cutlet. Transfer to a large plate.
2. Mix together all remaining ingredients.
3. Spread over fish.
4. Cover with cling wrap. Puncture twice with the tip of a knife to prevent a build-up of steam underneath. (See page 8.)
5. Cook at full power for 4 minutes.
6. Stand 1 minute. Uncover. Serve.

Watts	Full Power	Defrost
400	5 mins 20 secs	Nil
500	4 mins 40 secs	Nil
600	4 mins	Nil
650	3 mins 40 secs	Nil
700	3 mins 20 secs	Nil

VERY PLAIN PLAICE

Preparation — easy

Simple in style, quick to prepare and perfect with new potatoes and peas.

5 to 6 oz (150 to 175 g) frozen plaice fillets, *still frozen*
butter or margarine

1. Put fish on to a plate.
2. Spread with butter or margarine as though fish were a slice of bread.
3. Cover with cling wrap. Puncture twice with the tip of a knife to prevent a build-up of steam underneath. (See page 8.)
4. Cook at full power for 3½ minutes.
5. Stand 1 minute. Uncover. Serve.

Watts	Full Power	Defrost
400	4 mins 40 secs	Nil
500	4 mins 5 secs	Nil
600	3 mins 30 secs	Nil
650	3 mins 15 secs	Nil
700	2 mins 55 secs	Nil

STUFFED PLAICE PACK

Preparation — quick

Only four ingredients are necessary to make this chic main course which teams successfully with cauliflower, broccoli or a fresh green salad tossed with French dressing.

1 plaice fillet weighing 6 oz or 175 g
⅓ can (full weight 210 g) vegetable salad
2 teaspoons butter or margarine
paprika

1. Wash and dry fish.
2. Stand on a plate, skin side facing.
3. Arrange vegetable salad along one side of fillet. Fold over other half.
4. Put butter or margarine in a cup. Melt, uncovered, at defrost setting for ½ minute.
5. Spoon over fish. Sprinkle with paprika.
6. Cover with cling wrap. Puncture twice with the tip of a knife to prevent a build-up of steam underneath. (See page 8.)
7. Cook at full power for 3 minutes.
8. Stand for 1 minute. Uncover. Serve.

Watts	Full Power	Defrost
400	4 mins	40 secs
500	3 mins 30 secs	35 secs
600	3 mins	30 secs
650	2 mins 45 secs	28 secs
700	2 mins 30 secs	25 secs

LEMON SKATE WITH MUSHROOMS

Preparation — requires a bit of effort

Skate is a splendid specimen of fishhood and turns up trumps when cooked with lemon, butter and mushrooms as below. It is made for creamy mash and a dish of sprouts or cabbage.

1 piece of skate wing (fan-shaped), weighing about 5 oz or 150 g
2 oz (50 g) button mushrooms
½ oz (15 g) butter or margarine
2 teaspoons lemon juice
¼ level teaspoon salt
2 level teaspoons toasted breadcrumbs

1. Wash and dry skate. Transfer to a large plate.
2. Wash and dry mushrooms. Slice thinly. Arrange round fish.
3. Place butter or margarine in a cup. Melt, uncovered, at defrost setting for 1 minute. Stir in lemon juice and salt.
4. Spoon over fish. Sprinkle with crumbs.
5. Cover with cling wrap. Puncture twice with the tip of a knife to prevent a build-up of steam underneath. (See page 8.)
6. Cook at full power for 3¾ to 4 minutes.
7. Stand 1 minute. Uncover. Serve.

Watts	Full Power	Defrost
400	4 mins 55 secs to 5 mins 20 secs	1 min 20 secs
500	4 mins 20 secs to 4 mins 40 secs	1 min 10 secs
600	3 mins 45 secs to 4 mins	1 min
650	3 mins 25 secs to 3 mins 40 secs	55 secs
700	3 mins 10 secs to 3 mins 20 secs	50 secs

DEVILLED SKATE

Preparation — fairly quick and trouble-free

Classic skate is often poached and served with black butter sauce laced with capers. This is a more up-to-date rendering with a spectacular flavour. It needs brown rice sprinkled with crushed bran flakes to accompany and some buttered cauliflower dusted with the merest trace of nutmeg.

1 piece of skate wing (fan-shaped), weighing 7 oz or 200 g
½ oz (15 g) butter or margarine
1 teaspoon Worcestershire sauce
1 teaspoon malt vinegar
1 or 2 shakes of Tabasco
¼ level teaspoon salt

1. Wash and dry skate. Put on to a large plate.
2. Place butter or margarine in a cup. Melt, uncovered, at defrost setting for about 1 minute.
3. Stir in remaining ingredients. Spoon over skate.
4. Cover with cling wrap. Puncture twice with the tip of a knife to prevent a build-up of steam underneath. (See page 8.)
5. Cook at full power for 3½ minutes.
6. Stand 1 minute. Uncover. Serve.

Watts	Full Power	Defrost
400	4 mins 40 secs	1 min 20 secs
500	4 mins 5 secs	1 min 10 secs
600	3 mins 30 secs	1 min
650	3 mins 15 secs	55 secs
700	2 mins 55 secs	50 secs

SKATE WITH ORANGE AND CORIANDER

Preparation — needs a bit of your time

Wonderfully perfumed and an original way of preparing skate. Serve it with Indian Basmati rice and a dish of mango chutney.

---
1 piece of skate wing (fan-shaped), weighing 7 oz or 200 g

½ oz (15 g) butter or margarine

3 tablespoons fresh orange juice

2 slightly rounded tablespoons fresh coriander leaves, cut into shreds

---

1. Wash cod and put on to a plate.
2. Place butter or margarine into a cup.
3. Melt, uncovered, at defrost setting for about 1 minute.
4. Stir in orange juice.
5. Spoon over skate. Sprinkle with coriander.
6. Cover with cling wrap. Puncture twice with the tip of a knife to prevent a build-up of steam underneath. (See page 8.)
7. Cook at full power for 3½ minutes.
8. Stand 1 minute. Uncover. Serve.

Watts	Full Power	Defrost
400	4 mins 40 secs	1 min 20 secs
500	4 mins 5 secs	1 min 10 secs
600	3 mins 30 secs	1 min
650	3 mins 15 secs	55 secs
700	2 mins 55 secs	50 secs

MUSTARDY MUSHROOM COD

Preparation — reasonably fast

A little bit across the Channel in style, no French housewife would baulk at serving this meal of cod. It has a warm flavour, is light yet filling at the same time, and is low in cholesterol. Accompany with brown or green pasta.

8 oz (225 g) fillet of cod, cut from thick end
2 oz (50 g) mushrooms
½ oz (15 g) sunflower margarine
1 peeled and crushed garlic clove or ½-inch (1.25 gm) tubed garlic purée (optional)
1 level teaspoon French mustard
1 tablespoon milk
⅛ teaspoon salt

1. Wash cod and put on to a plate.
2. Trim, wash and slice mushrooms. Scatter over fish.
3. Transfer rest of ingredients to a small bowl.
4. Leave uncovered. Heat at defrost setting for 1½ minutes.
5. Spoon over fish.
6. Cover with cling wrap. Puncture twice with the tip of a knife to prevent a build-up of steam underneath. (See page 8.)
7. Cook at full power for 4 minutes.
8. Stand 1 minute. Uncover. Serve.

Watts	Full Power	Defrost
400	5 mins 20 secs	2 min
500	4 mins 40 secs	1 min 45 secs
600	4 mins	1 min 30 secs
650	3 mins 40 secs	1 min 25 secs
700	3 mins 10 secs	1 min 15 secs

POSH COD

Preparation — easy

A hearty portion to sate a good appetite, here is a hot meal 'par excellence'. It sits in its own overcoat of orangey-coloured cheese sauce and enjoys the company of almost any potato dish. Also garden peas.

1 cod steak weighing 8 oz or 225 g

1 pack (about 2¼ oz or 62.5 g) cream cheese with garlic and herbs

1 oz (25 g) deep yellow Cheddar cheese, grated

1 level tablespoon tomato ketchup

1 level tablespoon crushed corn flakes

1. Wash and dry fish.
2. Put into a 1 pint (575 ml) round cooking dish.
3. Mix together both cheeses. Spread over fish. Trickle tomato ketchup over the top.
4. Cover with cling wrap. Puncture twice with the tip of a knife to prevent a build-up of steam underneath. (See page 8.) Alternatively, use matching lid.
5. Cook on full power for 5 minutes.
6. Stand 1 minute. Uncover. Sprinkle with corn flakes. Serve.

Watts	Full Power	Defrost
400	6 mins 40 secs	Nil
500	5 mins 50 secs	Nil
600	5 mins	Nil
650	4 mins 35 secs	Nil
700	4 mins 10 secs	Nil

COD BONNE FEMME

Preparation — a bit fiddly

This translates from the French into the good-wife's cod and is packed with flavour and Gallic taste. Accompany with anything you fancy — potatoes, rice or fresh pasta and one green vegetable for colour.

1 cod steak weighing 8 oz or 225 g
1 oz (25 g) butter or margarine
2 oz (50 g) whole frozen baby onions, used from frozen
1 oz (25 g) button mushrooms, trimmed and sliced
1½ oz (40 g) unsmoked and lean bacon, chopped
chopped parsley for garnish

1. Wash and dry fish. Leave aside temporarily.
2. Put butter into a 1 pint (575 ml) round cooking dish. Melt, uncovered, at defrost setting for about 1½ minutes.
3. Mix in onions, mushrooms and bacon.
4. Cover with cling wrap. Puncture twice with the tip of a knife to prevent a build-up of steam underneath. (See page 8.) Alternatively, use matching lid.
5. Cook at full power for 2 minutes.
6. Uncover. Add fish. Coat with onion mixture. Re-cover.
7. Cook at full power for 4½ minutes.
8. Stand 2 minutes. Uncover. Sprinkle with parsley. Serve.

Watts	Full Power	Defrost
400	2 mins 40 secs; 5 mins 55 secs	2 mins
500	2 mins 20 secs; 5 mins 15 secs	1 min 45 secs
600	2 mins; 4 mins 30 secs	1 min 30 secs
650	1 min 50 secs; 4 mins 10 secs	1 min 25 secs
700	1 min 40 secs; 3 mins 45 secs	1 min 15 secs

COD WITH COCONUT AND CURRY

Preparation — reasonably fast

Slight overtones of the Far East are apparent in this slightly exotic cod dish. Serve with rice, mango chutney and a simple lettuce salad.

8 oz (225 g) fillet of cod, cut from thick end
¹⁄₂ oz (15 g) butter or margarine
¹⁄₂ level teaspoon medium strength curry powder
1 level tablespoon desiccated coconut
1 tablespoon milk
¹⁄₄ level teaspoon salt

1. Wash cod and put on to a plate.
2. Transfer rest of ingredients to a small bowl. Leave uncovered.
3. Heat at defrost setting for 1 minute.
4. Spoon over fish.
5. Cover with cling wrap. Puncture twice with the tip of a knife to prevent a build-up of steam underneath. (See page 8.)
6. Cook at full power for 3½ minutes.
7. Stand 1 minute. Uncover. Serve.

Watts	Full Power	Defrost
400	4 mins 40 secs	1 min 20 secs
500	4 mins 5 secs	1 min 10 secs
600	3 mins 30 secs	1 min
650	3 mins 15 secs	55 secs
700	2 mins 55 secs	50 secs

Jugged Kipper Fillet/Old Fashioned Herring/Perfectly Natural Christmas Pudding

Pasta Creme/Tortellini in Clear Soup

Tex-Mex Chili Chicken with Avocado/Devilled Pork

Potato Waffle/Californian Tofu Salad/Maple and Pecan Pudding

COLEY VINAIGRETTE

Preparation — effortless

A cordial main course, compatible with boiled or creamed potatoes plus one or two seasonal vegetables.

> **8 oz (225 g) fillet of coley, cut from thick end**
> **2 tablespoons bottled vinaigrette dressing**
> **6 fresh tarragon leaves**

1. Wash fish and put on to a plate.
2. Coat with vinaigrette dressing. Top with tarragon leaves.
3. Cover with cling wrap. Puncture twice with the tip of a knife to prevent a build-up of steam underneath. (See page 8.)
4. Cook at full power for 3½ minutes.
5. Stand 1 minute. Uncover. Serve.

Watts	Full Power	Defrost
400	4 mins 40 secs	Nil
500	4 mins 5 secs	Nil
600	3 mins 30 secs	Nil
650	3 mins 15 secs	Nil
700	2 mins 55 secs	Nil

'JUGGED' KIPPER FILLET

Preparation — a doddle

Kipper like it used to be in the old days when it was actually cooked by being stood in a jug of hot water. The only difference here is that the kipper is permitted to lie down in comfort and tastes all the better for it.

1 kipper fillet, weighing about 6 oz or 175 g
cold water
butter or margarine

1.   Choose a dish measuring 8 by 8 by 2 inches (20 by 20 by 5 cm).
2.   Wash kipper fillet. Put into dish. Cover with water.
3.   Cover with cling wrap. Puncture twice with the tip of a knife to prevent a build-up of steam underneath. (See page 8.)
4.   Cook at full power for 6 minutes.
5.   Stand 2 minutes. Strain. Put on to plate. Top with butter or margarine.

Watts	Full Power	Defrost
400	8 mins	Nil
500	7 mins	Nil
600	6 mins	Nil
650	5 mins 30 secs	Nil
700	5 mins	Nil

POACHED SMOKED HADDOCK

Preparation — needs a little attention

Traditionally British, what could better a piece of smoked haddock or cod, cooked in water and topped with a poached egg?

4 oz (125 g) fillet of smoked haddock or cod, cut from thick end
½ pt (275 ml) cold water
poached egg (page 00)

1. Wash fish. Put into a 1 pint (575 ml) cooking dish or bowl.
2. Add half the water.
3. Cover with cling wrap. Puncture twice with the tip of a knife to prevent a build-up of steam underneath. (See page 8.) Alternatively, use matching lid.
4. Cook at full power for 3 minutes. Uncover. Drain.
5. To remove excess saltiness, add rest of water and re-cover as above.
6. Cook at full power for another 2 minutes. Drain. Put on to a plate. Serve with butter, margarine or a poached egg (page 109) on top. Eat while hot.

Watts	Full Power	Defrost
400	4 mins; 2 mins 40 secs	Nil
500	3 mins 30 secs; 2 mins 20 secs	Nil
600	3 mins; 2 mins	Nil
650	2 mins 45 secs; 1 min 50 secs	Nil
700	2 mins 30 secs; 1 min 40 secs	Nil

FISH AND POTATO PIE

Preparation — needs attention

A simple but tasty little meal which is made with down-to-earth coley and flavoured with chives.

6 oz (175 g) potatoes
2 tablespoons water
½ level teaspoon salt
1 teaspoon butter or magarine
1 tablespoon milk
1 tablespoon chopped chives
8 oz (225 g) fillet of fresh coley, cut from thickest part
¼ level teaspoon salt
1 tablespoon water
1 heaped tablespoon crushed potato crisps

1. Peel potatoes, cut into chunks and wash. Put into a 1 pint (575 ml) round cooking dish.
2. Add water and salt. Cover with cling wrap. Puncture twice with the tip of a knife to prevent a build-up of steam underneath. (See page 8.) Alternatively, use matching lid.
3. Cook at full power for 4 minutes. Drain. Mash finely with butter or margarine and milk. Mix in chives. Leave aside for the moment.
4. Wash coley and put into a dish. Sprinkle with salt. Add water.
5. Cover as above. Cook 3 minutes at full power. Drain. Flake up flesh. Combine with potatoes.
6. Clean round sides of dish with kitchen paper towels. Sprinkle with crisps.
7. Leave uncovered. Reheat at full power for 1½ minutes. Stand 1 minute. Serve.

Watts	Full Power	Defrost
400	5 mins 20 secs; 4 mins; 2 mins	Nil
500	4 mins 40 secs; 3 mins 30 secs; 1 min 45 secs	Nil
600	4 mins; 3 mins; 1 min 30 secs	Nil
650	3 mins 40 secs; 2 mins 45 secs; 1 min 25 secs	Nil
700	3 mins 20 secs; 2 mins 30 secs; 1 min 15 secs	Nil

POULTRY, GAME AND MEAT

All recipes have been tested in a 600 watt oven.
See chart under each for variations of wattage.

MAGYAR CHICKEN

Preparation — time-consuming

An attempt to re-create the splendours of an old-time Hungarian classic. Eat with small pasta such as shells or wheels and accompany with green peas or beans — or both. I have used dried vegetables for ease.

1 x 5 oz (150 g) chicken breast, boned, skin removed
1 level tablespoon mixed dried peppers
1 level tablespoon dried sliced mushrooms
1 level tablespoon dried sliced onions
6 tablespoons boiling water
½ carton (2½ oz or 71 g) soured cream
1 level tablespoon tomato purée
1 level teaspoon paprika
1 level teaspoon salt
shake of pepper

1. Wash and dry chicken. Cut into fairly narow strips with a sharp knife or kitchen scissors. Leave aside for the moment.
2. Put dry vegetables into a 1 pint (575 ml) round cooking dish. Stir in water.
3. Cover with cling wrap. Puncture twice with the tip of a knife to prevent a build-up of steam underneath. (See page 8.) Alternatively, use matching lid.
4. Cook at defrost setting for 5 minutes then stand 4 minutes.
5. Top with chicken strips. Cover as above. Cook at full power for 2 minutes.
6. Beat together remaining ingredients.
7. Spread over chicken. Re-cover. Cook at defrost setting for 3 minutes.
8. Stand 3 minutes. Uncover. Stir round and serve.

Watts	Full Power	Defrost
400	2 mins 40 secs	6 mins 40 secs; 4 mins
500	2 mins 20 secs	5 mins 50 secs; 3 mins 30 secs
600	2 mins	5 mins; 3 mins
650	1 mins 50 secs	4 mins 35 secs; 2 mins 45 secs
700	1 min 40 secs	4 mins 10 secs; 2 mins 30 secs

HUNTERS' CHICKEN

Preparation — easy

A warm-hearted dish with a robust flavour. Eat with spaghetti or ribbon noodles. No extra vegetables are necessary.

1 x 7 oz (200 g) chicken breast with bone, skin removed
¼ level teaspoon garlic salt
1 can (7 oz or 200 g) button mushrooms, drained
6 black olives (optional)
4 oz (125 g) tomatoes, chopped
1 teaspoon Worcestershire sauce
¼ level teaspoon salt

1. Wash and dry chicken. Put into a 1 pint (575 ml) round cooking dish. Sprinkle with garlic salt.
2. Cover with cling wrap. Puncture twice with the tip of a knife to prevent a build-up of steam underneath. (See page 8.) Alternatively, use matching lid.
3. Cook at full power for 3½ minutes.
4. Uncover. Sprinkle with mushrooms, olives if used, tomatoes, Worcestershire sauce and salt.
5. Re-cover. Cook at full power for 1½ minutes.
6. Stand 2 minutes. Uncover. Serve.

Watts	Full Power	Defrost
400	4 mins 40 secs; 2 mins	Nil
500	4 mins 5 secs; 1 min 45 secs	Nil
600	3 mins 30 secs; 1 min 30 secs	Nil
650	3 mins 15 secs; 1 min 25 secs	Nil
700	2 mins 55 secs; 1 min 15 secs	Nil

CHICKEN STEW

Preparation — attention-seeking

With a genuine old-fashioned flavour, this is a prize for the discerning gourmet and is most at home with freshly cooked rice and sweetcorn kernels. Also with broccoli sprinkled with grated Cheddar cheese.

5 oz (150 g) chicken breast fillet, without bone
1½ oz (40 g) back bacon
2 oz (50 g) washed and dried courgettes, thinly sliced
2 oz (50 g) mushrooms
1 level teaspoon cornflour
1 level teaspoon stock or gravy granules
4 tablespoons water
½ level teaspoon salt

1. Wash and dry chicken.
2. Cut into strips and put into a 1 pint (575 ml) round cooking dish.
3. Chop bacon. Add to chicken.
4. Add sliced courgettes.
5. Trim and wash mushrooms. Cut into strips. Stir into chicken and bacon with rest of ingredients. Mix well.
6. Cover with cling wrap. Puncture twice with the tip of a knife to prevent a build-up of steam underneath. (See page 8.) Alternatively, use matching lid.
7. Cook at full power for 4½ minutes.
8. Stand 1½ minutes. Uncover. Stir round thoroughly and serve.

Watts	Full Power	Defrost
400	5 mins 55 secs	Nil
500	5 mins 15 secs	Nil
600	4 mins 30 secs	Nil
650	4 mins 10 secs	Nil
700	3 mins 45 secs	Nil

CHICKEN À LA KING

Preparation — easy

A toned-down version of a very popular North American dish, usually eaten with a warmed-up plain scone, rice or potatoes. It is another of those indulgence meals.

1 x 7 oz (220 g) chicken breast with bone, skin removed
1 level tablespoon mixed dried peppers
1 level tablespoon sliced mushrooms
1½ level teaspoons cornflour
2 tablespoons medium sherry
5 tablespoons cold milk
¼ level teaspoon salt

1. Wash and dry chicken. Put into a 1 pint (575 ml) round cooking dish.
2. Sprinkle with peppers and mushrooms.
3. Cover with cling wrap. Puncture twice with the tip of a knife to prevent a build-up of steam underneath. (See page 8.) Alternatively, use matching lid.
4. Cook at full power for 3½ minutes.
5. Mix cornflour smoothly with sherry. Stir in milk and salt.
6. Uncover chicken. Coat with cornflour mixture. Re-cover as before. Cook at full power for 2 minutes.
7. Stand 3 minutes. Uncover. Serve.

Watts	Full Power	Defrost
400	4 mins 40 secs; 2 mins 40 secs	Nil
500	4 mins 5 secs; 2 mins 20 secs	Nil
600	3 mins 30 secs; 2 mins	Nil
650	3 mins 15 secs; 1 min 50 secs	Nil
700	2 mins 55 secs; 1 min 40 secs	Nil

MOCK CHICKEN KIEV

Preparation — requires a modicum of your time

Rather grand, this one, and way up in the haute cuisine class. Serve it with new potatoes and French or sliced green beans. Or any crunchy salad to taste.

1 x 7 oz (200 g) chicken breast with bone, skin removed
¼ level teaspoon salt
½ oz (15 g) butter or margarine
1 heaped tablespoon chopped parsley
1 garlic clove, peeled
2 teaspoons lemon juice

1. Wash and dry chicken. Put into a 1 pint (575 ml) round cooking dish.
2. Sprinkle with salt.
3. Put butter or margarine into a small cup. Melt about 1 minute at defrost setting.
4. Stir in parsley then either grate or crush in the garlic. Add lemon juice, mix well and pour over the chicken.
5. Cover with cling wrap. Puncture twice with the tip of a knife to prevent a build-up of steam underneath. (See page 8.) Alternatively, use matching lid.
6. Cook at full power for 3½ minutes.
7. Stand 2 minutes. Uncover. Serve.

Watts	Full Power	Defrost
400	4 mins 40 secs	1 min 20 secs
500	4 mins 5 secs	1 min 10 secs
600	3 mins 30 secs	1 min
650	3 mins 15 secs	55 secs
700	2 mins 55 secs	50 secs

MALAY-STYLE CHICKEN

Preparation — requires a bit of effort

Authentically flavoured and quite delicious, eat this with rice or pasta tossed with a little butter or margarine. Green peas make a colourful accompaniment.

> **2 chicken thighs (8 oz or 225 g)**
> **3 level tablespoons peanut butter**
> **¼ level teaspoon paprika**
> **¼ level teaspoon garlic salt**
> **1 level tablespoon desiccated coconut**
> **5 tablespoons milk**
> **1 tablespoon lemon juice**

1. Wash and dry chicken. Slash flesh in 2 places with a sharp knife. Put into a 1 pint (575 ml) round cooking dish.
2. Cover with cling wrap. Puncture twice with the tip of a knife to prevent a build-up of steam underneath. (See page 8.) Alternatively, use matching lid.
3. Cook at full power for 4 minutes.
4. Meanwhile, mix together peanut butter, paprika, garlic salt, coconut and milk in small basin.
5. Remove chicken from microwave and leave to stand for 2 minutes..
6. Coat with peanut mixture. Cook, uncovered, at defrost setting for 3 minutes. Stir well.
7. Re-cover. Cook 2 minutes at full power. Stir in lemon juice.
8. Stand 5 minutes. Uncover. Serve.

Watts	Full Power	Defrost
400	5 mins 20 secs; 2 mins 40 secs	4 mins
500	4 mins 40 secs; 2 mins 20 secs	3 mins 30 secs
600	4 mins; 2 mins	3 mins
650	3 mins 40 secs; 1 min 50 secs	2 mins 45 secs
700	3 mins 20 secs; 1 min 40 secs	2 mins 30 secs

CHICKEN WITH A HINT OF PROVENCE

Preparation — demanding

Just the thing to recapture memories of a Mediterranean holiday. Serve with Risotto (page 00) and a salad of mixed lettuces, smartly tossed with French dressing.

1 oz (25 g) butter or margarine
4 oz (125 g) carrots, peeled and chopped
4 oz (125 g) onions, peeled and chopped
2 oz (50 g) celery, well-scrubbed and chopped
1 x 5 oz (150 g) chicken breast, boned, skin removed
1 small can (7 to 8 oz or 225 to 250 g) tomatoes, mashed in liquid
½ level teaspoon salt
pepper to taste
½ level teaspoon mixed herbs
black olives to garnish (optional)

1. Put butter or margarine into a 6 inch (15 cm) square cooking dish, 2 inches (5 cm) deep.
2. Melt, uncovered, at defrost setting for about 1 minute.
3. Mix in vegetables. Cook, uncovered, at full power for 3 minutes.
4. Wash and dry chicken. Slash flesh in 2 places with a sharp knife. Arrange on top.
5. Coat with tomatoes. Sprinkle with salt, pepper and herbs.
6. Cover with cling wrap. Puncture twice with the tip of a knife to prevent a build-up of steam underneath. (See page 8.) Alternatively, use matching lid.
7. Cook at full power for 7 minutes.
8. Stand 5 minutes. Uncover. Garnish with olives or leave plain. Serve.

Watts	Full Power	Defrost
400	4 mins 30 secs; 9 mins 15 secs	1 min 20 secs
500	3 mins 30 secs; 8 mins 5 secs	1 min 10 secs
600	3 mins; 7 mins	1 mins
650	2 mins 45 secs; 6 mins 25 secs	55 secs
700	2 mins 30 secs; 5 mins 55 secs	50 secs

SLIMMER'S CHICKEN CHOICE

Preparation — child's play

A beauty for dieters — moist, tender and appetising. Accompany with sprouts, cauliflower, broccoli or spinach and a slice of brown bread.

> 2 chicken thighs (8 oz or 225 g), skinned
> ¼ level teaspoon paprika
> 1 level teaspoon stock or gravy granules
> 2 teaspoons hot water
> 2 pickled onions (about 1 oz or 25 g)

1. Wash and dry chicken. Put into a 1 pint (575 ml) round cooking dish.
2. Sprinkle with paprika.
3. Mix stock or gravy granules with water. Pour round chicken.
4. Top with onions, first thinly sliced.
5. Cover with cling wrap. Puncture twice with the tip of a knife to prevent a build-up of steam underneath. (See page 8.) Alternatively, use matching lid.
6. Cook at full power for 5 minutes.
7. Stand 2 minutes. Uncover. Serve.

Watts	Full Power	Defrost
400	6 mins 40 secs	Nil
500	5 mins 50 secs	Nil
600	5 mins	Nil
650	4 mins 35 secs	Nil
700	4 mins 10 secs	Nil

CURRIED CHICKEN IN SPICY CARROT SAUCE

Preparation — requires a bit of effort

Completely off-beat, this is a colourful 'invention' of mine which works effortlessly in the microwave. Serve with rice and a side dish of chutney.

> 2 chicken thighs (8 oz or 225 g)
> ½ to 1 level teaspoon medium strength curry powder
> 1 can (7 oz or 200 g) carrots
> ⅛ teaspoon ground ginger
> ⅛ teaspoon garlic or onion salt
> ⅛ teaspoon plain salt
> ½ level teaspoon cornflour
> 1 tablespoon milk

1. Wash and dry chicken. Put into a 1 pint (575 ml) round cooking dish.
2. Sprinkle with curry powder.
3. Cover with cling wrap. Puncture twice with the tip of a knife to prevent a build-up of steam underneath. (See page 8.) Alternatively, use matching lid.
4. Cook at full power for 4½ minutes.
5. Meanwhile, drain carrots and mash very finely. Stir in rest of ingredients.
6. Uncover chicken. Spread with carrot mixture. Re-cover as above. Cook at full power for 1½ minutes.
7. Stand 4 minutes. Uncover. Serve.

Watts	Full Power	Defrost
400	5 mins 55 secs; 2 mins	Nil
500	5 mins 15 secs; 1 min 45 secs	Nil
600	4 mins 30 secs; 1 min 30 secs	Nil
650	4 mins 10 secs; 1 min 25 secs	Nil
700	3 mins 45 secs; 1 min 15 secs	Nil

SOY CHICKEN

Preparation — fairly quick and trouble-free

A dish with a wonderful flavour and crispy texture. It's made for a noodle accompaniment.

3 oz (75 g) soya sprouts
3 spring onions
2 chicken thighs (8 oz or 225 g)
1 rounded teaspoon stock or gravy granules
2 tablespoons boiling water
shake of pepper

1. Wash and drain soya sprouts. Trim and chop spring onions.
2. Put into a 1 pint (575 ml) round cooking dish.
3. Wash and dry chicken. Place on top.
4. Mix together granules and water. Add pepper.
5. Pour over chicken mixture.
6. Cover with cling wrap. Puncture twice with the tip of a knife to prevent a build-up of steam underneath. (See page 8.) Alternatively, use matching lid.
7. Cook at full power for 6 minutes.
8. Stand 4 minutes. Uncover. Serve.

Watts	Full Power	Defrost
400	8 mins	Nil
500	7 mins	Nil
600	6 mins	Nil
650	5 mins 30 secs	Nil
700	5 mins	Nil

TROPICAL CHICKEN

Preparation — a bit fiddly

A lavish portion with a spectacular flavour. It is designed for winter when Sharon fruit* and fresh dates are in season. Serve with spaghetti or mashed potatoes and any extra vegetable to taste.

2 chicken drumsticks (8 oz or 225 g)
1 Sharon fruit (4 oz or 125 g)
paprika
⅛ level teaspoon salt
2 rounded tablespoons mango chutney
1 fresh date, skinned and halved

1. Wash and dry drumsticks. Slash flesh in 3 places with a sharp knife.
2. Wash and dry Sharon fruit. Slice fairly thinly and arrange over base of large plate, keeping it in the centre.
3. Stand drumsticks on top, fleshy parts facing edge of plate.
4. Sprinkle with paprika and salt then top with chutney.
5. Add halved date.
6. Cover with cling wrap. Puncture twice with the tip of a knife to prevent a build-up of steam underneath. (See page 8.)
7. Cook at full power for 6 minutes.
8. Stand 5 minutes. Uncover. Serve.

Watts	Full Power	Defrost
400	8 mins	Nil
500	7 mins	Nil
600	6 mins	Nil
650	5 mins 30 secs	Nil
700	5 mins	Nil

* An Israeli hybrid, related to the persimmon but less astringent.

SWEET-SOUR CHICORY CHICKEN

Preparation — a bit fiddly

A fun dish, this, with a flavour all its own. Serve with rice or noodles and a salad of soya or bean sprouts.

> **2 chicken drumsticks (8 oz or 225 g)**
> **1 head of chicory (4 oz or 125 g), trimmed and washed**
> **1 oz (25 g) celery, well washed**
> **1 tablespoon soy sauce**
> **1 tablespoon vinegar**
> **1 tablespoon honey, at kitchen temperature**

1. Wash and dry drumsticks. Slash flesh in 3 places with a sharp knife.
2. Stand on large plate, fleshy parts facing edge.
3. Remove 'core' of chicory at root end as this can be quite bitter. Cut chicory in half lengthwise. Stand on either side of drumsticks.
4. Cut celery into thin slices. Place in between drumsticks.
5. Beat together soy sauce, vinegar and honey.
6. Pour over drumsticks.
7. Cover with cling wrap. Puncture twice with the tip of a knife to prevent a build-up of steam underneath. (See page 8.)
8. Cook at full power for 7 minutes.
9. Stand 5 minutes. Uncover. Serve.

Watts	Full Power	Defrost
400	9 mins 15 secs	Nil
500	8 mins 5 secs	Nil
600	7 mins	Nil
650	6 mins 25 secs	Nil
700	5 mins 55 secs	Nil

TEX-MEX CHILI CHICKEN WITH AVOCADO

Preparation — requires a bit of effort

A personal favourite, to be enjoyed by all lovers of Mexican-style food which is catching on fast in the UK. Accompany with tortilla chips (packeted) and, for added fibre, a dish of red kidney beans warmed in the microwave. Wonderful.

2 chicken drumsticks (8 oz or 225 g)
1 medium sized ripe avocado
2 teaspoons Taco Sauce
1 teaspoon lemon juice
4 oz (125 g) washed and chopped tomatoes
½ level teaspoon salt

1. Wash and dry drumsticks. Slash flesh in 3 places with a sharp knife.
2. Put into a 6 inch (15 cm) square cooking dish, 2 inches (5 cm) deep.
3. Cover with cling wrap. Puncture twice with the tip of a knife to prevent a build-up of steam underneath. (See page 8.) Alternatively, use matching lid.
4. Cook at full power for 4 minutes.
5. Meanwhile, halve avocado and scoop flesh into a bowl. Mash down well with Taco sauce and lemon juice.
6. Uncover chicken. Coat with avocado mixture. Top with tomatoes. Sprinkle with salt.
7. Re-cover. Cook at full power for 1½ minutes.
8. Stand 4 minutes. Uncover. Serve.

Watts	Full Power	Defrost
400	5 mins 20 secs; 2 mins	Nil
500	4 mins 40 secs; 1 min 45 secs	Nil
600	4 mins; 1 min 30 secs	Nil
650	3 mins 40 secs; 1 min 25 secs	Nil
700	3 mins 20 secs; 1 min 15 secs	Nil

CHICKEN WITH A DASH OF FIRE

Preparation — requires a bit of effort

A zippy dish which does much to add sparkle to chicken drumsticks. The sauce looks as though it were made from cottage cheese but nothing of the sort; the effect comes about through yoghurt and the extras added to it. It's meant for broccoli and creamed potatoes, if only packet mash.

2 chicken drumsticks (8 oz or 225 g)
3 heaped tablespoons thick set, natural yoghurt
1 level teaspoon creamed horseradish
1 level teaspoon Dijon mustard
½ level teaspoon paprika
½ level teaspoon onion salt
1 heaped tablespoon chopped parsley or toasted cashew nuts

1. Wash and dry drumsticks. Slash flesh in 3 places with a sharp knife.
2. Put into a 1 pint (575 ml) cooking dish.
3. Cover with cling wrap. Puncture twice with the tip of a knife to prevent a build-up of steam underneath. (See page 8.) Alternatively, use matching lid.
4. Cook at full power for 4 minutes.
5. Meanwhile, mix all remaining ingredients, except parsley or nuts, well together.
6. Uncover chicken. Coat with yoghurt mixture.
7. Re-cover. Cook at full power for 1½ minutes.
8. Stand 5 minutes. Uncover. Sprinkle with parsley or nuts. Serve.

Watts	Full Power	Defrost
400	5 mins 20 secs; 1 min 45 secs	Nil
500	4 mins 40 secs; 1 min 35 secs	Nil
600	4 mins; 1 min 30 secs	Nil
650	3 mins 40 secs; 1 min 25 secs	Nil
700	3 mins 20 secs; 1 min 15 secs	Nil

SPOIL YOURSELF CHICKEN WITH MUSHROOMS AND PORT

Preparation — fairly quick and trouble-free

Indulgent and why not. Serve with potato waffles, heated in the microwave, or any other ready-prepared frozen potato dish. Accompany with canned carrots or a salad of grated carrots tossed with French dressing and mustard and cress.

2 chicken drumsticks (8 oz or 225 g)
¼ level teaspoon onion salt
pepper to taste
¼ level teaspoon paprika
⅛ level teaspoon dried thyme
3 oz (75 g) washed and dried mushrooms, sliced
2 tablespoons port

1. Wash and dry drumsticks. Slash flesh in 3 places with a sharp knife.
2. Put into a 1 pint (575 ml) cooking dish.
3. Sprinkle with onion salt, pepper, paprika and thyme.
4. Cover with cling wrap. Puncture twice with the tip of a knife to prevent a build-up of steam underneath. (See page 8.) Alternatively, use matching lid.
5. Cook at full power for 4 minutes.
6. Uncover. Surround with mushrooms. Coat with port.
7. Re-cover. Cook at full power for 2 minutes.
8. Stand 5 minutes. Uncover. Serve.

Watts	Full Power	Defrost
400	5 mins 20 secs; 2 mins 40 secs	Nil
500	4 mins 40 secs; 2 mins 20 secs	Nil
600	4 mins; 2 mins	Nil
650	3 mins 40 secs; 1 min 50 secs	Nil
700	3 mins 20 secs; 1 min 40 secs	Nil

A TRY AT CHICKEN 'STIR-FRY'

Preparation — easy and straightforward

A marvellous compromise. Chinese in temperament, low in fat and very well-flavoured. And *no* frying which can't be done in the microwave anyway.

4 oz courgettes, washed and dried
3 large spring onions
1 x 5 oz (150 g) chicken breast with bone, skin removed
1 tablespoon soy sauce

1.   Top and tail courgettes. Thinly slice. Put into a 1 pint (575 ml) round cooking dish.
2.   Trim spring onions and chop. Sprinkle over courgettes.
3.   Wash and dry chicken. Slash flesh in 2 places with a sharp knife. Place on courgettes.
4.   Coat with soy sauce.
5.   Cover with cling wrap. Puncture twice with the tip of a knife to prevent a build-up of steam underneath. (See page 8.) Alternatively, use matching lid.
6.   Cook at full power for 3½ minutes.
7.   Stand 3 minutes. Uncover. Serve.

Watts	Full Power	Defrost
400	4 mins 40 secs	Nil
500	4 mins 5 secs	Nil
600	3 mins 30 secs	Nil
650	3 mins 15 secs	Nil
700	2 mins 55 secs	Nil

COMFORTING CHICKEN WING BROTH WITH RICE

Preparation — easy

Imagine, on a cold winter's day, being able to cook a warming, main course soup meal in ten minutes. This takes no more and is a splendid brew for insulation.

2 chicken wings (7 oz or 200 g)
1 level tablespoon easy-cook, long grain rice
1 level tablespoon dried sliced onions
1 level tablespoon dried parsley or fresh chopped if preferred
¼ pt (150 ml) hot water
1 level teaspoon stock or gravy granules
⅛ level teaspoon salt
shake of pepper

1. Wash and dry wings. Put into a 1 pint (575 ml) soup bowl.
2. Cover with cling wrap. Puncture twice with the tip of a knife to prevent a build-up of steam underneath. (See page 8.)
3. Cook at full power for 2½ minutes. Stand 2 minutes. Uncover.
4. Add rice, onions, parsley and water mixed with gravy granules.
5. Pour over wings. Sprinkle with salt and pepper.
6. Re-cover as above. Cook at defrost setting for 7 minutes.
7. Stand 3 minutes. Uncover. Serve.

Watts	Full Power	Defrost
400	3 mins 20 secs	9 mins 15 secs
500	2 mins 55 secs	8 mins 5 secs
600	2 mins 30 secs	7 mins
650	2 mins 20 secs	6 mins 25 secs
700	2 mins 5 secs	5 mins 55 secs

SPRINGTIME TURKEY

Preparation — fairly quick and trouble-free

Something one might expect to find in a French provincial town, this is warming, soothing, flavourful and in perfect harmony with freshly made toast or heated-up garlic bread.

6 oz (175 g) turkey breast fillet, weighed without bone

1 level tablespoon flour

3 pickled onions in brown vinegar, thinly sliced

1 can (7 oz or 198 g) petit pois

2 tablespoons milk

¼ to ½ level teaspoon salt

2 level tablespoons crushed potato crisps

1. Cut turkey fillet into small cubes.
2. Put into a 1 pint (575 ml) round cooking dish. Stir in flour and onions.
3. Cover with cling wrap. Puncture twice with the tip of a knife to prevent a build-up of steam underneath. (See page 8.) Alternatively, use matching lid.
4. Cook at full power for 3 minutes.
5. Uncover. Stir in petit pois and liquid from can, milk and salt. Mix thoroughly.
6. Re-cover as above. Cook at full power for 2 minutes.
7. Stand 2 minutes. Uncover. Stir round. Sprinkle with crisps. Serve.

Watts	Full Power	Defrost
400	4 mins; 2 mins 40 secs	Nil
500	3 mins 30 secs; 2 mins 20 secs	Nil
600	3 mins; 2 mins	Nil
650	2 mins 45 secs; 1 min 50 secs	Nil
700	2 mins 30 secs; 1 min 40 secs	Nil

TURKEY IN A WOOD

Preparation — fairly quick and trouble-free

Distinguished in taste and fairly classy, this seems a much more expensive meal than it is. It is tasty with brown rice and sweetcorn.

6 oz (175 g) turkey breast fillet, weighed without bone
4 oz (125 g) trimmed leek (1 medium)
1 level tablespoon flour
1 can (7.76 oz or 220 g) prunes in syrup
¼ to ½ level teaspoon salt

1. Cut turkey fillet into small cubes.
2. Put into a 1 pint (575 ml) round cooking dish. Slit leek, thoroughly wash and cut into thin slices.
3. Stir into turkey with flour.
4. Cover with cling wrap. Puncture twice with the tip of a knife to prevent a build-up of steam underneath. (See page 8.) Alternatively, use matching lid.
5. Cook at full power for 4 minutes.
6. Uncover. Stir in prunes, syrup from can and salt. Mix thoroughly.
7. Re-cover as above. Cook at full power for 2 minutes.
8. Stand 2 minutes. Uncover. Stir round and serve.

Watts	Full Power	Defrost
400	5 mins 20 secs; 2 mins 40 secs	Nil
500	4 mins 40 secs; 2 mins 20 secs	Nil
600	4 mins; 2 mins	Nil
650	3 mins 40 secs; 1 min 50 secs	Nil
700	3 mins 20 secs; 1 min 40 secs	Nil

NORMANDY TURKEY

Preparation — attention-seeking

Very French, very chic and heartily-flavoured. It's bliss with brown noodles (the flat kind) and Brussels sprouts. And the garlic makes it the perfect dish for eating when you're on your own and out of contact with the rest of the human race.

6 oz (175 g) boneless turkey breast fillet, weighed without bone

½ oz (15 g) butter or margarine

1 garlic clove, peeled and crushed

1 level tablespoon cornflour

¼ level teaspoon salt

1 level teaspoon stock or gravy granules

½ level teaspoon powder mustard

8 tablespoons dry cider

1. Wash and dry turkey. Cut into strips.
2. Put butter or margarine into a 1 pint (575 ml) round cooking dish.
3. Melt, uncovered, at defrost setting for about 1 minute.
4. Mix in garlic and turkey. Cover with cling wrap. Puncture twice with the tip of a knife to prevent a build-up of steam underneath. (See page 8.) Alternatively, use matching lid.
5. Cook at full power for 3 minutes.
6. Mix cornflour, salt, stock or gravy granules and the mustard smoothly with the cider.
7. Uncover turkey. Coat with cider mixture. Stir in well.
8. Re-cover. Cook at full power for 3 minutes.
9. Stand 3 minutes. Uncover. Stir round and serve.

Watts	Full Power	Defrost
400	4 mins; 4 mins	1 min 20 secs
500	3 mins 30 secs; 3 mins 30 secs	1 min 10 secs
600	3 mins; 3 mins	1 min
650	2 mins 45 secs; 2 mins 45 secs	55 secs
700	2 mins 30 secs; 2 mins 30 secs	50 secs

TURKEY IN THE PINK

Preparation — attention-seeking

A swish dish when you feel like a touch of class and splendid with broccoli and creamed potatoes.

6 oz (175 g) turkey breast fillet, weighed without bone
½ oz (15 g) butter or margarine
1½ oz (40 g) onion, peeled and chopped
1 level tablespoon cornflour
¼ level teaspoon salt
¼ level teaspoon paprika
8 tablespoons rosé wine

1. Wash and dry turkey. Cut into small cubes.
2. Put butter or margarine into a 1 pint (575 ml) round cooking dish.
3. Melt, uncovered, at defrost setting for about 1 minute.
4. Stir in onion and turkey. Cover with cling wrap. Puncture twice with the tip of a knife to prevent a build-up of steam underneath. (See page 00.) Alternatively, use matching lid.
5. Cook at full power for 3 minutes.
6. Mix cornflour, salt, paprika and wine smoothly together in a basin. Gradually and smoothly blend in wine.
7. Uncover turkey. Coat with wine mixture.
8. Re-cover. Cook at full power for 3 minutes.
9. Stand 3 minutes. Uncover. Stir round and serve.

Watts	Full Power	Defrost
400	4 mins; 4 mins	1 min 20 secs
500	3 mins 30 secs; 3 mins 30 secs	1 min 10 secs
600	3 mins; 3 mins	1 min
650	2 mins 45 secs; 2 mins 45 secs	55 secs
700	2 mins 30 secs; 2 mins 30 secs	50 secs

LIME RABBIT

Preparation — no hassle

With home-produced rabbit appearing in the shops more often than it used to, it is well worth cooking in the microwave for a fairly economical and unusual meal. This version is especially tempting with green noodles and heated-up canned carrots tossed with butter or margarine.

8 oz (225 g) pieces of fresh rabbit
2 oz (50 g) onion, peeled and sliced
1½ level teaspoons cornflour
½ small bottle Perrier with natural lime flavour
1 level teaspoon stock or gravy granules
1 tablespoon hot water
⅛ teaspoon salt

1. Wash and dry rabbit.
2. Put into a 1 pint (575 ml) round cooking dish. Top with sliced onion.
3. Cover with cling wrap. Puncture twice with the tip of a knife to prevent a build-up of steam underneath. (See page 8.) Alternatively, use matching lid.
4. Cook at full power for 3½ minutes.
5. Mix together cornflour, Perrier water, stock or gravy granules. Blend smoothly with hot water and the salt.
6. Uncover rabbit. Pour in Perrier liquid.
7. Re-cover. Cook at full power for 3½ minutes.
8. Stand 3 minutes. Uncover. Serve.

Watts	Full Power	Defrost
400	4 mins 40 secs; 4 mins 40 secs	Nil
500	4 mins 5 secs; 4 mins 4 secs	Nil
600	3 mins 30 secs; 3 mins 30 secs	Nil
650	3 mins 15 secs; 3 mins 15 secs	Nil
700	2 mins 55 secs; 2 mins 55 secs	Nil

RABBIT IN MUSTARD SAUCE

Preparation — a doddle

Creamy-rich and ritzy, this is a classic way of preparing rabbit. It's made for brown rice and a zippy lettuce salad.

8 oz (225 g) pieces of fresh rabbit
2 level teaspoons cornflour
1 level teaspoon powder mustard
¼ level teaspoon salt
1 slightly rounded tablespoon tomato ketchup
¼ pt (150 ml) milk

1. Wash and dry rabbit.
2. Put into a 1 pint (575 ml) round cooking dish.
3. Cover with cling wrap. Puncture twice with the tip of a knife to prevent a build-up of steam underneath. (See page 8.) Alternatively, use matching lid.
4. Cook at full power for 3 minutes.
5. Mix cornflour, mustard and salt together in a bowl. Gradually blend in ketchup, followed by milk. Ensure mixture is smooth.
6. Uncover rabbit. Coat with the mustard mixture.
7. Re-cover. Cook at full power for 3 minutes.
8. Stand 3 minutes. Uncover. Serve.

Watts	Full Power	Defrost
400	4 mins; 4 mins	Nil
500	3 mins 30 secs; 3 mins 30 secs	Nil
600	3 mins; 3 mins	Nil
650	2 mins 45 secs; 2 mins 45 secs	Nil
700	2 mins 30 secs; 2 mins 30 secs	Nil

MEAT DISHES

Because salt has a toughening effect on some meat dishes, it has been added *after* the completion of cooking. This is clearly specified in each recipe.

MINCED BEEF STEW

Preparation — easy

This beauty cunningly uses prepared coleslaw mix (sold in supermarkets) to let you off the hook where peeling, chopping, slicing and grating of fresh veg are concerned. It goes well with rice, packet mash or hunks of fresh brown bread.

4 oz (125 g) lean minced beef
3 oz (75 g) coleslaw mix (minus any sort of dressing)
1 level teaspoon stock or gravy granules
¼ pt (150 ml) hot water
pepper to taste

1. Put mince into a 1 pint (575 ml) round cooking dish. Add coleslaw. Mix in well.
2. Cover with cling wrap. Puncture twice with the tip of a knife to prevent a build-up of steam underneath. (See page 8.) Alternatively, use matching lid.
3. Cook at full power for 2 minutes. Uncover.
4. Mix together last 3 ingredients. Stir well into mince and vegetables.
5. Re-cover as above. Cook at full power for 2 minutes.
6. Stand 1½ minutes. Uncover. Stir round and serve.

Watts	Full Power	Defrost
400	2 mins 40 secs; 2 mins 40 secs	Nil
500	2 mins 20 secs; 2 mins 20 secs	Nil
600	2 mins; 2 mins	Nil
650	1 min 50 secs; 1 min 50 secs	Nil
700	1 min 40 secs; 1 min 40 secs	Nil

STEWED MINCE WITH VEGETABLES

Preparation — easy

A cold weather dish which is compatible with potatoes or rice and cabbage or sprouts. It has an appetising flavour and deep bronze colour.

4 oz (125 g) lean minced beef
2 level teaspoons plain flour
1 level tablespoon dried sliced onions
1 level tablespoon dried sliced mushrooms
1 slightly rounded teaspoon stock or gravy granules
¼ pt (150 ml) boiling water
salt and pepper to taste

1. Mix meat with flour and dried vegetables. Transfer to a 1 pint (575 ml) round cooking dish.
2. Cover with cling wrap. Puncture twice with the tip of a knife to prevent a build-up of steam underneath. (See page 8.) Alternatively, use matching lid.
3. Cook at full power for 2 minutes. Uncover. Break up well with a fork.
4. Stir in stock or gravy granules dissolved in the water.
5. Cover as above. Cook at full power for 3¼ minutes.
6. Stand 2 minutes. Uncover. Season to taste. Stir round and serve.

Watts	Full Power	Defrost
400	2 mins 40 secs; 4 mins 15 secs	Nil
500	2 mins 20 secs; 3 mins 45 secs	Nil
600	2 mins; 3 mins 15 secs	Nil
650	1 min 50 secs; 3 mins	Nil
700	1 min 40 secs; 2 mins 45 secs	Nil

CURRIED MINCE

Preparation — fairly fast

A simple curry for those who appreciate well-flavoured food. I admit it isn't authentic but it makes a pleasing meal with rice and chutney and responds speedily to microwave treatment.

4 oz (125 g) lean minced beef
2 level tablespoons dried mixed vegetables
1 level teaspoon flour
1 level teaspoon stock or gravy granules
1½ level teaspoons medium strength curry powder
¼ pt (150 ml) hot water

1. Put mince into a 1 pint (575 ml) round cooking dish. Mix in vegetables and flour.
2. Cover with cling wrap. Puncture twice with the tip of a knife to prevent a build-up of steam underneath. (See page 8.) Alternatively, use matching lid.
3. Cook at full power for 3 minutes. Uncover.
4. Combine remaining ingredients well together. Fork into mince.
5. Re-cover as above. Cook at full power for 2 minutes.
6. Stand 1½ minutes. Uncover. Stir round and serve.

Watts	Full Power	Defrost
400	4 mins; 2 mins 40 secs	Nil
500	3 mins 30 secs; 2 mins 20 secs	Nil
600	3 mins; 2 mins	Nil
650	2 mins 45 secs; 1 min 50 secs	Nil
700	2 mins 30 secs; 1 min 40 secs	Nil

SPEEDY BOLOGNESE SAUCE

Preparation — requires a bit of effort

The *only* partner for this true-to-life sauce is spaghetti, although noodles and pasta shells are acceptable.

4 oz (125 g) lean minced beef
1 level tablespoon dried sliced onions
1 level tablespoon dried sliced mushrooms
1 level tablespoon mixed dried peppers
½ level teaspoon mixed herbs
2 level teaspoons flour
1 level teaspoon stock or gravy granules
2 tablespoons hot water or red wine at room temperature
1 small can (7 to 8 oz or 200 to 225 g) tomatoes
salt and pepper to taste

1. Mix meat with dried vegetables, herbs and flour.
2. Transfer to a 1 pint (575 ml) round cooking dish.
3. Leave uncovered. Cook at full power for 2 minutes.
4. Break up well with a fork.
5. Stir in stock or gravy granules mixed with wine or water.
6. Crush tomatoes and add.
7. Cover with cling wrap. Puncture twice with the tip of a knife to prevent a build-up of steam underneath. (See page 8.) Alternatively, use matching lid.
8. Cook at full power for 4 minutes.
9. Stand 2 minutes. Uncover. Season to taste. Stir round. Serve with pasta.

Watts	Full Power	Defrost
400	2 mins 40 secs; 5 mins 20 secs	Nil
500	2 mins 20 secs; 4 mins 40 secs	Nil
600	2 mins; 4 mins	Nil
650	1 min 50 secs; 3 mins 40 secs	Nil
700	1 min 40 secs; 3 mins 20 secs	Nil

MEAT STUFFED PEPPER

Preparation — requires a bit of effort

Always popular, the pepper is ready to eat in ten minutes and is a complete meal in itself.

1 large red or green pepper (8 oz or 225 g)
4 oz (125 g) raw minced meat, beef, veal, pork or lamb
1 level tablespoon easy-cook, long grain rice
½ level teaspoon onion salt
1 level teaspoon stock or gravy granules
3 tablespoons hot water
¼ level teaspoons mixed herbs
To cook
1 level teaspoon stock or gravy granules
3 tablespoons hot water

1. Wash and dry pepper. Cut off top, keep for lid and remove inside fibres and seeds. If necessary, cut a thin sliver off the base of the pepper so that it stands upright without toppling over.
2. Mix together next 6 ingredients. Pack into pepper. Top with lid.
3. Stand in a 1 pint (575 ml) basin. Add stock or gravy granules mixed with water.
4. Cover with cling wrap. Puncture twice with the tip of a knife to prevent a build-up of steam underneath. (See page 8.)
5. Cook at full power for 6 minutes.
6. Stand 4 minutes. Uncover. Serve.

Tip
Pepper retains a certain appetising crispness.

Watts	Full Power	Defrost
400	8 mins	Nil
500	7 mins	Nil
600	6 mins	Nil
650	5 mins 30 secs	Nil
700	5 mins	Nil

MINCED MEAT GOULASH

Preparation — fairly quick and trouble-free

Characterfully and colourfully Hungarian, this is a beauty of a dish for leisured cooking. Eat it with tiny pasta and accompany with a swig now and then of deep red Bull's Blood wine.

6 oz (175 g) minced veal or pork
2 level tablespoons dried sliced onions
2 level tablespoons mixed dried peppers
½ level tablespoon flour
1 small can (about 7 to 8 oz or 200 to 225 g) tomatoes
½ level teaspoon paprika
¾ level teaspoon salt
2 slightly rounded tablespoons soured cream

1. Put meat into a 1 pint (575 ml) round cooking dish. Mash in onions, peppers and flour.
2. Cover with cling wrap. Puncture twice with the tip of a knife to prevent a build-up of steam underneath. (See page 8.) Alternatively, use matching lid.
3. Cook at full power for 3 minutes. Break up meat with a fork.
4. Crush in the tomatoes. Add paprika. Re-cover as above. Cook at full power for 2 minutes.
5. Stand 2 minutes. Uncover. Stir in salt and cream. Serve.

Watts	Full Power	Defrost
400	4 mins; 2 mins 40 secs	Nil
500	3 mins 30 secs; 2 mins 20 secs	Nil
600	3 mins; 2 mins	Nil
650	2 mins 45 secs; 1 min 50 secs	Nil
700	2 mins 30 secs; 1 min 40 secs	Nil

THE QUARTER POUNDER BURGER

Preparation — easy

A classic burger and just the kind to pop into a round bun with a spread of mustard or ketchup. It takes no longer to make and cook than a ready-prepared frozen one and can be eaten with pickles and salad.

4 oz (125 g) lean minced beef
1 level tablespoon plain flour
¼ level teaspoon salt
1 tablespoon milk

1. Thoroughly mix beef with remaining ingredients.
2. Shape into a 3½ inch (9 cm) round burger.
3. Transfer to a plate.
4. Cook, uncovered, at full power for 2 minutes.
5. Stand 1 minute. Serve.

Watts	Full Power	Defrost
400	2 mins 40 secs	Nil
500	2 mins 20 secs	Nil
600	2 mins	Nil
650	1 min 50 secs	Nil
700	1 min 40 secs	Nil

TANDOORI QUARTER POUNDER BURGER

Make exactly as The Quarter Pounder Burger, adding ½ level teaspoon Tandoori spice mix to the beef mixture. The cooking time stays the same.

THE QUARTER POUNDER CHEESEBURGER

Make as The Quarter Pounder Burger. After burger has cooked and stood for 1 minute, cover with ½ oz (15 g) slice of processed cheese. Cook on full power for about ½ minute.

Watts	Full Power	Defrost
400	40 secs	Nil
500	35 secs	Nil
600	30 secs	Nil
650	28 secs	Nil
700	25 secs	Nil

JUMBO BURGER

Preparation — easy

A feast for hungry eyes, this is a hunk of a juicy burger which is at its happiest with coleslaw or potato salad, mixed pickles and fresh bread. Also chips which you can buy if you happen to live near a fish and chip shop.

8 oz (225 g) coarse-cut raw minced beef, extra lean
⅛ teaspoon onion salt
1 rounded tablespoon packeted crusty white breadcrumbs
1 tablespoon milk
1 level teaspoon stock or gravy granules
lettuce leaves
cut-up tomato

1. Put meat into a bowl. Add the next 4 ingredients.
2. Mix thoroughly. Shape into a 4½ inch (11 cm) round burger.
3. Transfer to a large plate. Leave uncovered.
4. Cook at full power for 4 minutes.
5. Stand 2 minutes. Add lettuce and tomato. Serve.

Tip
The burger creates its own gravy.

Watts	Full Power	Defrost
400	5 mins 20 secs	Nil
500	4 mins 40 secs	Nil
600	4 mins	Nil
650	3 mins 40 secs	Nil
700	3 mins 20 secs	Nil

JUMBO CHEESEBURGER

Make as Jumbo burger. After burger has cooked and stood for 2
minutes, cover with about 1½ oz (40 g) sliced processed cheese. Cook
on full power for about ¾ to 1 minute until melted. Serve straightaway.

Watts	Full Power	Defrost
400	1 min to 1 min 20 secs	Nil
500	55 secs to 1 min 10 secs	Nil
600	45 secs to 1 min	Nil
650	40 secs to 55 secs	Nil
700	35 secs to 50 secs	Nil

DIETER'S ONION BEEFBURGER

Preparation — a doddle

Simple, plain and unpretentious — just the thing for dieters if they
dress up the burger with a dollop of low-calorie salad cream or natural
yogurt and eat it with salad.

4 oz (125 g) coarse cut raw minced beef, extra lean

1 level teaspoon plain or onion Bisto

1. Mix meat and Bisto well together.
2. Shape into a 3½ inch (9 cm) round burger.
3. Carefully transfer to a plate.
4. Cook, uncovered, at full power for 1½ minutes.
5. Stand 1 minute. Serve.

DIETER'S MUSTARD BEEFBURGER

Make exactly as Dieter's Onion Beefburger, adding 1 level teaspoon prepared mild mustard to the beef and Bisto.

Watts	Full Power	Defrost
400	2 mins	Nil
500	1 min 45 secs	Nil
600	1 min 30 secs	Nil
650	1 min 25 secs	Nil
700	1 min 15 secs	Nil

OATY VEAL BURGER

Preparation — easy

A tasty burger which goes well with potato waffles or chips and heated up processed peas. At least that's how I like it.

4 oz (125 g) minced veal
2 level tablespoons porridge oats
¼ level teaspoon stock or gravy granules
⅛ level teaspoon salt
2 tablespoons milk

1. Mix all ingredients well together.
2. Shape into a 3½ inch (9 cm) round burger.
3. Transfer to a plate.
4. Cook, uncovered, at full power for 2½ minutes.
5. Stand 1 minute. Serve.

Watts	Full Power	Defrost
400	3 mins 20 secs	Nil
500	2 mins 55 secs	Nil
600	2 mins 30 secs	Nil
650	2 mins 20 secs	Nil
700	2 mins 5 secs	Nil

CORNED BEEF HASH

Preparation — requires a bit of effort

Just a few ingredients to make one of the tastiest North American classics of all time.

8 oz (225 g) potatoes
2½ tablespoons hot water
¼ level teaspoon salt
1 rounded teaspoon butter or margrine
4 oz (125 g) corned beaf, broken up
1 tablespoon milk
½ level teaspoon prepared mustard

1. Peel potatoes, wash and cut into small pieces.
2. Put into roomy serving bowl with water. Sprinkle with salt.
3. Cover with cling wrap. Puncture twice with the tip of a knife to prevent a build-up of steam underneath. (See page 8.)
4. Cook until tender at full power for 6 to 7 minutes.
5. Drain. Mash well with butter or margarine.
6. Add corned beef, milk and mustard. Mash in well. Clean up edges of dish with kitchen paper.
7. Cover with cling wrap as above.
8. Cook at full power for 2 minutes.
9. Stand 1 minute. Uncover. Serve from the bowl.

Watts	Full Power	Defrost
400	8 mins to 9 mins 15 secs; 2 mins 40 secs	Nil
500	7 mins to 8 mins 5 secs; 2 mins 20 secs	Nil
600	6 mins to 7 mins; 2 mins	Nil
650	5 mins 30 secs to 6 mins 25 secs; 1 min 50 secs	Nil
700	5 mins to 5 mins 55 secs; 1 min 40 secs	Nil

Corned Beef Hash with Egg

Make exactly as above then top hot Hash with a poached egg (See page 109).

VEAL CASSEROLE IN CHICKEN SAUCE

Preparation — needs a bit of your time

A pleasing dish, made from diced veal which is usually available from large supermarket chains. Eat with coleslaw or green salad and either rice or pasta.

> **7 oz (200 g) diced veal**
> **1 small can (4.9 oz or 140 g) condensed cream of chicken soup**
> **1 heaped tablespoon crushed crisps or toasted flaked almonds**

1. Wash and dry veal.
2. Cut up into small pieces so that veal looks like chunky mince.
3. Arrange, in a ring, in a 1 pint (575 ml) round cooking dish.
4. Cover with cling wrap. Puncture twice with the tip of a knife to prevent a build-up of steam underneath. (See page 8.) Alternatively, use matching lid.
5. Cook at full power for 2½ minutes.
6. Uncover. Stir in soup. Re-cover. Cook at defrost setting for 2 minutes.
7. Uncover. Stir round. Sprinkle with crisps or almonds. Eat from the dish.

Watts	Full Power	Defrost
400	3 mins 20 secs	2 mins 40 secs
500	2 mins 55 secs	2 mins 20 secs
600	2 mins 30 secs	2 mins
650	2 mins 20 secs	1 min 50 secs
700	2 mins 5 secs	1 min 40 secs

'BARBECUED' RIB BONES

Preparation — reasonably fast

Moist and succulent with plenty of gravy, these flavoursome ribs are ideal for an evening alone when you can munch the bones and lick your fingers without anyone seeing. Eat with pitta bread.

3 or 4 pork rib bones (8 to 9 oz or 225 to 250 g)
2 slightly rounded teaspoons orange marmalade
2 teaspoons vinegar
2 teaspoons soy sauce
⅛ level teaspoon salt

1. Wash and dry ribs. Arrange on a plate like spokes of a wheel.
2. Put rest of ingredients into a cup. Warm through at defrost setting for about ½ to ¾ minute.
3. Spoon over ribs.
4. Cover with cling wrap. Puncture twice with the tip of a knife to prevent a build-up of steam underneath. (See page 8.)
5. Cook at full power for 4½ minutes.
6. Stand 1 minute. Uncover. Serve.

Watts	Full Power	Defrost
400	5 mins 55 secs	40 secs to 1 min
500	5 mins 15 secs	35 secs to 55 secs
600	4 mins 30 secs	30 secs to 45 secs
650	4 mins 10 secs	28 secs to 40 secs
700	3 mins 45 secs	25 secs to 35 secs

SUNNY-TOPPED RIBS

Preparation — child's play

Very tasty and made for garlic bread or crusty rolls, first warmed through in the microwave.

3 or 4 pork ribs (8 to 9 oz or 225 to 250 g)
1 level tablespoon tomato purée
1 level teaspoon creamed horseradish
½ level teaspoon French mustard

1. Wash and dry ribs. Arrange on a plate like spokes of a wheel.
2. Mix together next 3 ingredients.
3. Spread over ribs.
4. Cover with cling wrap. Puncture twice with the tip of a knife to prevent a build-up of steam underneath. (See page 8.)
5. Cook at full power for 4½ minutes.
6. Stand 1 minute. Uncover. Serve.

Watts	Full Power	Defrost
400	5 mins 55 secs	Nil
500	5 mins 15 secs	Nil
600	4 mins 30 secs	Nil
650	4 mins 10 secs	Nil
700	3 mins 45 secs	Nil

DEVILLED PORK

Preparation — easy

A zippy-tasting pork dish which goes well with sweetcorn, carrots and rice.

1 prime loin of pork chop, as lean as possible (6 to 7 oz or 175 go 200 g)
1 teaspoon Worcestershire sauce
1 level teaspoon tomato ketchup
1 level teaspoon brown ketchup
¼ to ½ level teaspoon curry powder
¼ level teaspoon salt
⅛ level teaspoon powder mustard

1. Wash and dry chop.
2. Transfer to a plate.
3. Beat together rest of ingredients.
4. Spread over chop.
5. Cover with cling wrap. Puncture twice with the tip of a knife to prevent a build-up of steam underneath. (See page 8.)
6. Cook at full power for 4 minutes.
7. Stand 1 minute. Uncover. Serve.

Watts	Full Power	Defrost
400	5 mins 20 secs	Nil
500	4 mins 40 secs	Nil
600	4 mins	Nil
650	3 mins 40 secs	Nil
700	3 mins 20 secs	Nil

GAMMON WITH LIME AND PEAR

Preparation — a bit fiddly

An amazingly good production — vaguely exotic and perfectly at home with cooked tomatoes and a jacket potato.

1 round, unsmoked gammon steak (about 8 oz or 225 g)
2 tablespoons lime cordial
5 tablespoons cold water
1 medium pear (3 oz or 75 g)

1. Snip gammon all the way round to prevent it from curling as it cooks.
2. Put into a 1 pint (575 ml) round cooking dish. Add water.
3. Cover with cling wrap. Puncture twice with the tip of a knife to prevent a build-up of steam underneath. (See page 8.) Alternatively, use matching lid.
4. Cook at full power for 3½ minutes. Drain. Transfer to a large plate.
5. Coat with lime cordial. Peel, quarter and core pear. Cut into slices. Arrange on top of gammon.
6. Cover with cling wrap as above. Cook at full power for 1 minute.
7. Stand 1½ minutes. Uncover. Serve.

Watts	Full Power	Defrost
400	4 mins 40 secs; 1 min 20 secs	Nil
500	4 mins 5 secs; 1 min 10 secs	Nil
600	3 mins 30 secs; 1 min	Nil
650	3 mins 15 secs; 55 secs	Nil
700	2 mins 55 secs; 50 secs	Nil

PORK IN A NEST

Preparation — hassle-free

If you've a healthy appetite, this is for you. Accompany with sprouts, cabbage or cauliflower — or all three.

1 can (7½ or 213 g) spaghetti in tomato sauce

1 prime loin of pork chop, as lean as possible (6 to 7 oz or 175 to 200 g)

¼ **level teaspoon mixed herbs**

¼ **level teaspoon paprika**

⅛ **level teaspoon salt**

1. Tip spaghetti into a 1 pint (575 ml) round cooking dish.
2. Top with washed and dried chop.
3. Sprinkle with rest of ingredients.
4. Cover with cling wrap. Puncture twice with the tip of a knife to prevent a build-up of steam underneath. (See page 8.) Alternatively, use matching lid.
5. Cook at full power for 5 minutes.
6. Stand 1½ minutes. Uncover. Serve.

Watts	Full Power	Defrost
400	6 mins 40 secs	Nil
500	5 mins 50 secs	Nil
600	5 mins	Nil
650	4 mins 35 secs	Nil
700	4 mins 10 secs	Nil

SAUSAGE CASSEROLE

Preparation — a doddle

For students everywhere, by special request. Eat with any bread to taste or jacket potatoes.

1 small can (7 to 8 oz or 200 to 225 g) tomatoes
1 level teaspoon cornflour
2 rounded tablespoons dried mixed vegetables
4 oz (125 g) pork or beef sausages, each cut into 5 chunks
seasoning to taste

1.   Crush tomatoes into a 1 pint (575 ml) round cooking dish.
2.   Mix in cornflour and the dried mixed vegetables.
3.   Cover with cling wrap. Puncture twice with the tip of a knife to prevent a build-up of steam underneath. (See page 8.) Alternatively, use matching lid.
4.   Cook at full power for 4 minutes.
5.   Uncover. Stir in sausages. Re-cover.
6.   Cook at full power for 3 minutes.
7.   Stand 2 minutes. Uncover. Season to taste. Stir round and serve.

Watts	Full Power	Defrost
400	5 mins 20 secs; 4 mins	Nil
500	4 mins 40 secs; 3 mins 30 secs	Nil
600	4 mins; 3 mins	Nil
650	3 mins 40 secs; 2 mins 45 secs	Nil
700	3 mins 20 secs; 2 mins 30 secs	Nil

LAMB KEBAB

Preparation — needs a modicum of patience

Beautifully tender lamb characterises this Oriental-style kebab and, because the metal skewer is well covered with meat, no harm will come to the microwave.

6 oz (175 g) neck of lamb fillet
1 level teaspoon stock or gravy granules
1 teaspoon boiling water
⅛ level teaspoon garlic powder

1. Wash and dry lamb. Cut into cubes. Thread on to a 6 inch (15 cm) skewer. Transfer to a plate.
2. Mix together remaining ingredients. Brush over meat.
3. Cover loosely with kitchen paper to prevent spluttering.
4. Cook at full power for 3 minutes.
5. Stand ½ minute. Uncover. Serve.

Watts	Full Power	Defrost
400	4 mins	Nil
500	3 mins 30 secs	Nil
600	3 mins	Nil
650	2 mins 45 secs	Nil
700	2 mins 30 secs	Nil

PIQUANT LAMB CUTLETS

Preparation — child's play

A relaxed pleasure for weekends. Eat with jacket potatoes and a buxom salad tossed with a sharpish dressing.

3 lamb cutlets (about 7 oz or 200 g), cut from best end neck

1 tablespoon brown ketchup

1. Wash and dry lamb.
2. Arrange cutlets on a plate like spokes of a wheel, fleshy ends towards edge of plate.
3. Spread with ketchup.
4. Cover loosely with kitchen paper to prevent spluttering.
5. Cook at full power for 3½ minutes.
6. Stand ½ minute. Uncover. Serve.

Watts	Full Power	Defrost
400	4 mins 40 secs	Nil
500	4 mins 5 secs	Nil
600	3 mins 30 secs	Nil
650	3 mins 15 secs	Nil
700	2 mins 55 secs	Nil

LIVER AND ONIONS

Preparation — no hassle

A golden oldie which adapts happily to the microwave and cries out for side dishes of potatoes and sprouts. My speedy short cut is using dried onions.

2 rounded tablespoons dried sliced onions

4 tablespoons water

4 oz (125 g) lamb's liver

1½ extra tablespoons water

1 rounded teaspoons stock or gravy granules

¼ to ½ level teaspoon salt

pepper to taste

1. Tip onions into a 1 pint (575 ml) round cooking dish. Mix in water.
2. Leave uncovered. Cook at full power for 1¾ minutes.
3. Wash and dry liver. Cut into strips.
4. Add to onions with extra water and the stock or gravy granules. Mix in well.
5. Cover with cling wrap. Puncture twice with the tip of a knife to prevent a build-up of steam underneath. (See page 8.) Alternatively, use matching lid.
6. Cook at full power for 3 minutes.
7. Stand 1 minute. Uncover. Add salt and pepper to taste. Stir round and serve.

Watts	Full Power	Defrost
400	2 mins 25 secs; 4 mins	Nil
500	2 mins 5 secs; 3 mins 30 secs	Nil
600	1 mins 45 secs; 3 mins	Nil
650	1 mins 35 secs; 2 mins 45 secs	Nil
700	1 mins 25 secs; 2 mins 30 secs	Nil

LIVER AND BACON BRAISE

Preparation — fairly quick and trouble-free

A friendly combination for any time of year. It's delicious with macaroni, quite filling and also nourishing.

4 oz (125 g) lamb's liver
2 oz (50 g) unsmoked back bacon
1 can (5.11 oz or 145 g) garden peas and liquor from can
1 slightly rounded teaspoon stock or gravy granules

1. Wash and dry liver. Cut into narrow strips.
2. Coarsely chop bacon. Put into a 1 pint (575 ml) round cooking dish.
3. Stir in liver, garden peas with can liquor, and the stock or gravy granules.
4. Cover with cling wrap. Puncture twice with the tip of a knife to prevent a build-up of steam underneath. (See page 8.) Alternatively, use matching lid.
5. Cook at full power for 4 minutes.
6. Stand 1½ minutes. Uncover. Stir round and serve.

Watts	Full Power	Defrost
400	5 mins 20 secs	Nil
500	4 mins 40 secs	Nil
600	4 mins	Nil
650	3 mins 40 secs	Nil
700	3 mins 20 secs	Nil

PEPPERCORN KIDNEYS

Preparation — needs a bit of your time

Anyone into kidneys will drool over this one with its slight peppery kick-back and zesty sauce. It's best on a slice of thick hot toast or spooned over a freshly baked and halved jacket potato.

2 very fresh lamb's kidneys
black peppercorns in mill
1 level teaspoon cornflour
1 teaspoon Worcestershire sauce
4 tablespoons cold water
¼ level teaspoon salt

1. Wash, dry and halve kidneys then cut into small dice.
2. Put into a 1 pint (575 ml) round cooking dish. Grind over a thin layer of pepper from mill.
3. Mix in rest of ingredients.
4. Cover with cling wrap. Puncture twice with the tip of a knife to prevent a build-up of steam underneath. (See page 8.) Alternatively, use matching lid.
5. Cook at full power for 3 minutes.
6. Stand 1 minute. Uncover. Stir round and serve.

Watts	Full Power	Defrost
400	4 mins	Nil
500	3 mins 30 secs	Nil
600	3 mins	Nil
650	2 mins 45 secs	Nil
700	2 mins 30 secs	Nil

COUNTRY KIDNEYS

Preparation -- needs a bit of your time

A happy marriage of ingredients makes this kidney meal a special attraction. Accompany with vegetables to taste or a salad.

> **2 very fresh lamb's kidneys**
> **2 oz (50 g) mushrooms**
> **1 level teaspoon cornflour**
> **¼ level teaspoon mixed herbs**
> **¼ level teaspoon salt**
> **¼ level teaspoon paprika**
> **5 tablespoons apple juice**

1. Wash, dry and halve kidneys then cut into small dice.
2. Trim and wash mushrooms. Cut into narrow strips.
3. Put both into a 1 pint (575 ml) round cooking dish.
4. Stir in remaining ingredients, mixing in well.
5. Cover with cling wrap. Puncture twice with the tip of a knife to prevent a build-up of steam underneath. (See page 8.) Alternatively, use matching lid.
6. Cook at full power for 3½ minutes.
7. Stand 1 minute. Uncover. Stir round and serve.

Watts	Full Power	Defrost
400	4 mins 40 secs	Nil
500	4 mins 5 secs	Nil
600	3 mins 30 secs	Nil
650	3 mins 15 secs	Nil
700	2 mins 55 secs	Nil

EGGS AND CHEESE

All recipes have been tested in a 600 watt oven.
See chart under each for variations of wattage.

CHEESE SAUCE FOR EVERYTHING

Preparation — fairly quick and trouble-free

A smooth, full-flavoured and creamy sauce, suitable for serving over vegetables, burgers, chicken and split jacket potatoes.

2 large slices (3 oz or 75 g) processed cheese
4 tablespoons milk
¼ teaspoon powder mustard
shake of pepper

1. Tear cheese slices into biggest pieces and put into a fairly small bowl.
2. Add milk, mustard and pepper to taste.
3. Put a plastic or stainless steel spoon into bowl
4. Cook, uncovered, at defrost setting for 4 minutes, stirring at the end of each minute.
5. Remove from oven, give a final brisk stir and use as required.

To Vary
SEASON WITH:
1 level teaspoon bottled Madagascar green peppers
1 level teaspoon chopped gherkins
1 level teaspoon chopped pickled onions or pickled walnuts
1 level teaspoon anchovy essence
2 level teaspoons fresh chopped parsley

Watts	Full Power	Defrost
400	Nil	4 mins 50 secs
500	Nil	4 mins 40 secs
600	Nil	4 mins
650	Nil	3 mins 40 secs
700	Nil	3 mins 20 secs

CHEESE ON TOAST

Preparation — fairly quick and trouble-free

A variation of the Cheese Sauce For Everything recipe, this is a thicker version and makes a super topping for a slice of freshly toasted bread — and a substantial snack.

2 large slices (3 oz or 75 g) processed cheese
2 tablespoons milk, cider or beer
¼ level teaspoon powder mustard
shake of pepper
1 large slice freshly made toast

1. Tear cheese slices into biggish pieces and put into a fairly small bowl.
2. Add milk, mustard and pepper to taste.
3. Put a plastic or stainless steel spoon into bowl.
4. Cook, uncovered, at defrost setting for 3 minutes, stirring at the end of each minute.
5. Remove from oven, give a final brisk stir and spread over a slice of toast already on a plate.
6. Reheat, uncovered, for 1½ to 2 minutes at defrost setting until hot and bubbly. Eat straightaway.

Watts	Full Power	Defrost
400	Nil	4 mins; 2 mins to 2 mins 40 secs
500	Nil	3 mins 30 secs; 1 min 45 secs to 2 mins 20 secs
600	Nil	3 mins; 1 min 30 secs to 2 mins
650	Nil	2 mins 45 secs; 1 min 25 secs to 1 min 50 secs
700	Nil	2 mins 30 secs; 1 min 15 secs to 1 min 40 secs

MOCK FRIED EGG

Preparation — very easy and quick

A velvety-smooth egg which turns up trumps and is certainly less greasy than one cooked conventionally.

1 Grade 2 egg
1 small, shallow and well-greased dish
salt and pepper to taste

1. Break egg gently into dish. Puncture yolk twice with the tip of a knife.
2. Sprinkle with salt and pepper. Cover dish with a plastic lid or plate.
3. Cook at full power for ¾ minute. Stand 1 minute.
4. Cook an extra 20 to 30 seconds when white should be set. If not, cook a few seconds longer.

Watts	Full Power	Defrost
400	1 min; 26 to 40 secs	Nil
500	55 secs; 23 to 35 secs	Nil
600	45 secs; 20 to 30 secs	Nil
650	40 secs 18 to 28 secs	Nil
700	35 secs; 17 to 25 secs	Nil

MOCK FRIED EGGS

. Use 2 eggs. Follow directions above but use cooking table below.

Watts	Full Power	Defrost
400	1 min 20 secs; 40 to 52 secs	Nil
500	1 min 10 secs; 35 to 46 secs	Nil
600	1 min; 30 to 40 secs	Nil
650	55 secs; 28 to 37 secs	Nil
700	50 secs; 25 to 34 secs	Nil

SOFT BOILED EGG

Preparation — child's play

Imagine boiling an egg in a cup and then turning it out onto a slice of toast. This is microwave wizardry at its most ingenious and bliss for breakfast.

1 Grade 2 egg, at kitchen temperature
teacup brushed with butter or margarine

1. Break egg into cup. Puncture yolk twice with the tip of a knife.
2. Cover with a saucer. Cook at defrost setting for 1 minute.
3. Gently twirl egg round in cup. Cook at defrost setting for further ½ minute. Stand ½ minute.

Watts	Full Power	Defrost
400	Nil	1 min 20 secs; 40 secs
500	Nil	1 min 10 secs; 35 secs
600	Nil	1 min; 30 secs
650	Nil	55 secs 28 secs
700	Nil	50 secs; 25 secs

MEDIUM SOFT BOILED EGG

Follow directions above but use cooking table below.

Watts	Full Power	Defrost
400	Nil	2 mins 40 secs; 40 secs
500	Nil	2 mins 20 secs; 35 secs
600	Nil	2 mins; 30 secs
650	Nil	1 min 50 secs; 28 secs
700	Nil	1 min 40 secs; 25 secs

HARD BOILED EGG

Follow directions for soft boiled egg but use cooking table below. Leave egg to stand for ¾ minute.

Watts	Full Power	Defrost
400	Nil	3 mins 20 secs; 40 secs
500	Nil	2 mins 55 secs; 35 secs
600	Nil	2 mins 30 secs; 30 secs
650	Nil	2 mins 20 secs; 28 secs
700	Nil	2 mins 5 secs; 25 secs

EGG MAYONNAISE

Preparation — very easy

Cook 1 hard boiled egg as directed on page 106. Leave until cold. Loosen edges and turn out on to a plate lined with lettuce. Coat with mayonnaise. Garnish with salad; spring onions, cucumber, tomatoes, celery, beetroot, pepper strips.

BASIC OMELET

Preparation — fairly easy and quick

It was my mother who taught me never to use a large pan for a small omelet. This applies equally to microwave cooking, so I've used a dessert dish (about 1 pint or 575 ml) and the omelet turns out thick, tender and moist.

knob of butter or margarine

2 Grade 2 eggs

¼ level teaspoon salt

2 teaspoons water

1. Put butter or margarine into dish as described above.
2. Melt at full power for ½ minute. Brush over inside of dish.
3. Beat rest of ingredients well together until light and frothy.
4. Pour into dish. Leave uncovered. Cook at full power for 1½ minutes. Stir round. Cook a further ½ minute when omelet will rise to top of dish.
5. Stand ½ minute. Turn out on to a plate. Serve.

Watts	Full Power	Defrost
400	40 secs; 2 mins; 40 secs	Nil
500	35 secs; 1 min 45 secs; 35 secs	Nil
600	30 secs; 1 min 30 secs; 30 secs	Nil
650	28 secs; 1 min 25 secs; 28 secs	Nil
700	25 secs; 1 min 15 secs; 25 secs	Nil

HERB OMELET

Make as above, adding 2½ level tablespoons chopped fresh herbs (parsley, tarragon, dill, chives etc.) to beaten eggs. Cook ¾ minute longer, following times below.

Watts	Full Power	Defrost
400	40 secs; 2 mins; 1 min	Nil
500	35 secs; 1 min 45 secs; 55 secs	Nil
600	30 secs; 1 min 30 secs; 45 secs	Nil
650	28 secs; 1 min 25 secs; 40 secs	Nil
700	25 secs; 1 min 15 secs; 35 secs	Nil

SCRAMBLED EGG

Preparation — almost effortless

The best ever — creamy, moist and superbly textured.

> 1 Grade 2 egg, at kitchen temperature
> 2 teaspoons milk
> pinch of salt

1. Beat egg thoroughly with milk and salt.
2. Pour into a greased teacup or small basin, preferably in clear glass.
3. Cover with a saucer. Cook at full power for ½ minute.
4. Stir round. Re-cover. Cook a further 15 seconds when egg should be lightly set and almost filling its container.
5. Uncover. Stir. Serve.

Watts	Full Power	Defrost
400	40 secs; 20 secs	Nil
500	35 secs; 18 secs	Nil
600	30 secs; 15 secs	Nil
650	28 secs; 14 secs	Nil
700	25 secs; 13 secs	Nil

SCRAMBLED EGGS

Use 2 eggs. Follow directions above but use cooking table below.

Watts	Full Power	Defrost
400	1 min; 33 secs	Nil
500	55 secs; 29 secs	Nil
600	45 secs; 25 secs	Nil
650	40 secs; 23 secs	Nil
700	35 secs; 21 secs	Nil

POACHED EGG

Preparation — almost effortless

A light egg dish without additional fat. Serve on toast or a toasted muffin.

6 tablespoons near boiling water

½ teaspoon malt vinegar

1 Grade 2 egg, at kitchen temperature

1. Pour water into a smallish dish. Add vinegar.
2. Gently break in the egg and puncture yolk twice with the tip of a knife.
3. Cover dish with a plastic lid or plate.
4. Cook 50 to 75 seconds, depending on how firm you like the white to be.
5. Remove from microwave. Stand 1 minute.
6. Lift out of dish with perforated spoon or fish slice. Serve.

Watts	Full Power	Defrost
400	1 min 5 secs to 1 min 35 secs	Nil
500	1 min to 1 min 25 secs	Nil
600	50 secs to 1 min 15 secs	Nil
650	45 secs to 1 min 10 secs	Nil
700	40 secs to 1 min 5 secs	Nil

VEGETABLES

All recipes have been tested in a 600 watt oven.
See chart under each for variations of wattage.

MASHED POTATOES

Preparation — easy

| 6 oz (175 g) potatoes |
| 2 tablespoons water |
| ½ level teaspoon salt |
| knob of butter or margarine |
| 1 tablespoon milk |

1. Peel potatoes, cut into chunks and wash. Put into a 1 pint (575 ml) round cooking dish.
2. Add water and salt. Cover with cling wrap. Puncture twice with the tip of a knife to prevent a build-up of steam underneath. (See page 8.) Alternatively, use matching lid.
3. Cook at full power for 4 minutes. Drain. Mash finely with butter or margarine and milk, adding a little extra milk for a lighter texture.
4. Tidy edges of dish. Reheat potatoes, uncovered, for ½ minute at full power.

Watts	Full Power	Defrost
400	5 mins 20 secs; 40 secs	Nil
500	4 mins 40 secs; 35 secs	Nil
600	4 mins; 30 secs	Nil
650	3 mins 40 secs; 28 secs	Nil
700	3 mins 20 secs; 25 secs	Nil

JACKET POTATO

Preparation — easy as pie

Jacket potatoes in the microwave are superb and one by itself takes only between 5 to 6 minutes to cook — like magic for speed.

1 medium potato (4 to 5 oz or 125 to 150 g)

1. Wash and dry potato. Prick in about 6 places with a fork.
2. Stand on a plate or a piece of kitchen paper.
3. Cover with paper.
4. Cook on full power for 5 to 6 minutes. Wrap in a clean teatowel. Stand for 5 minutes.
5. Split open. Fill with butter, margarine or soured cream.

Watts	Full Power	Defrost
400	6 mins 40 secs to 8 mins	Nil
500	5 mins 50 secs to 7 mins	Nil
600	5 to 6 mins	Nil
650	4 mins 35 secs to 5 mins 30 secs	Nil
700	4 mins 10 secs to 5 mins	Nil

JACKETS WITH BAKED BEANS

Cook potato as described above. Split open. Put on to a plate. Fill with 1 can (5.29 oz or 150 g) baked beans in tomato sauce. Leave uncovered and cook at full power for 2½ minutes.

Watts	Full Power	Defrost
400	3 mins 20 secs	Nil
500	2 mins 55 secs	Nil
600	2 mins 30 secs	Nil
650	2 mins 20 secs	Nil
700	2 mins 5 secs	Nil

CHEESEY JACKETS WITH TOMATO

Prepare potato as above. Split open. Put on to a plate. Fill with 2 oz (50 g) Cheddar cheese slices and 1 level tablespoon tomato ketchup. Leave uncovered and cook at full power for 1½ minutes.

Watts	Full Power	Defrost
400	2 mins	Nil
500	1 mins 45 secs	Nil
600	1 mins 30 secs	Nil
650	1 mins 25 secs	Nil
700	1 mins 15 secs	Nil

POTATO WAFFLE

Preparation — a doddle

Available everywhere now, frozen potato waffles go amiably with almost anything and cook fast and well in the microwave. Not crisp but still delicious.

1 frozen potato waffle

1. Place waffle on to a plate.
2. Leave uncovered.
3. Cook at full power for 1½ minutes, turning it over completely halfway through cooking.
4. Stand ¼ minute. Serve.

Watts	Full Power	Defrost
400	2 mins	Nil
500	1 min 45 secs	Nil
600	1 min 30 secs	Nil
650	1 min 25 secs	Nil
700	1 min 15 secs	Nil

PIZZA POTATOES

Preparation — a little demanding

What a delicious change from pizza on a bread base. The potatoes make an admirable substitute, in some ways lighter, and the dish can be deemed hearty with lots of good flavour. Certainly it's more than adequate for a main course and enjoys the company of a green salad tossed with French dressing.

9 oz (250 g) potatoes
2 tablespoons water
½ level teaspoon salt
2 tablespoons milk
knob of butter or margarine
2 oz (50 g) red Leicester cheese, grated
¼ level teaspoon dried basil
1 level tablespoon tomato ketchup
4 to 6 black olives (optional)

1. Peel and wash potatoes. Cut into chunks. Put into a 1 pint (575 ml) round serving dish.
2. Add water and salt. Stir round.
3. Cover with cling wrap. Puncture twice with the tip of a knife to prevent a build-up of steam underneath. (See page 8.)
4. Cook at full power for 6 minutes.
5. Uncover. Drain if necessary (sometimes no water remains).
6. Mash finely with milk and butter. Smooth top.
7. Sprinkle with cheese and basil. Drizzle ketchup over top.
8. Leave uncovered. Cook at full power for 1½ minutes. Garnish with olives if using. Serve.

Watts	Full Power	Defrost
400	8 mins; 2 mins	Nil
500	7 mins; 1 min 45 secs	Nil
600	6 mins; 1 min 30 secs	Nil
650	5 mins 30 secs; 1 min 25 secs	Nil
700	5 mins; 1 min 15 secs	Nil

ASPARAGUS IN BUTTER

Preparation — easy

For a special treat in May or June, cook yourself some asparagus and eat it hot with butter.

> **6 green asparagus spears, about 5 oz or 150 g**
> **2 tablespoons cold water**
> **¼ level teaspoon salt**

1. Cut about 1 inch (2.5 cm) off ends of asparagus.
2. Arrange spears in a long cooking dish. Take care not to damage tips.
3. Add water. Sprinkle with salt.
4. Cover with cling wrap. Puncture twice with the tip of a knife to prevent a build-up of steam underneath. (See page 8.) Alternatively, use matching lid.
5. Cook at full power for 6 minutes.
6. Stand 1 minute. Uncover and remove from dish. Eat hot with butter.

Watts	Full Power	Defrost
400	8 mins	Nil
500	7 mins	Nil
600	6 mins	Nil
650	5 mins 30 secs	Nil
700	5 mins	Nil

BROCCOLI WITH FRENCH FLAIR

Preparation — fairly easy

Anyone into the vegetarian scene will appreciate this continental-style broccoli, served on brown toast and sprinkled with flaked and toasted almonds. It makes a super lunch or supper dish.

6 oz (175 g) broccoli florets
3 tablespoons boiling water
1/4 level teaspoon salt
2 level teaspoons cornflour
7 tablespoons milk
1 pack (about 2 1/4 oz or 62.5 g) cream cheese with garlic and herbs
1/2 oz (15 g) flaked and toasted almonds

1. Wash broccoli and shake dry.
2. Put into a 1 pint (575 ml) round cooking dish.
3. Add water. Sprinkle with salt. Cover with cling wrap. Puncture twice with the tip of a knife to prevent a build-up of steam underneath. (See page 8.) Alternatively, use matching lid.
4. Cook on full power for 3 minutes.
5. Blend cornflour smoothly with milk. Gradually mix into the cream cheese.
6. Uncover and drain broccoli. Coat with the cheese mixture. Sprinkle with nuts.
7. Re-cover. Cook at full power for 2 1/2 minutes.
8. Stand 1 minute. Stir round. Spoon over hot toast. Serve.

Watts	Full Power	Defrost
400	4 mins; 3 mins 20 secs	Nil
500	3 mins 30 secs; 2 mins 55 secs	Nil
600	3 mins; 2 mins 30 secs	Nil
650	2 mins 45 secs; 2 mins 20 secs	Nil
700	2 mins 30 secs; 2 mins 5 secs	Nil

VEGETARIAN STUFFED PEPPER

Preparation — requires a bit of effort

An appetising mix of flavours makes this main course pepper dish eminently suitable for the non-meat eating brigade.

1 large red or green pepper (8 oz or 225 g)
1 level tablespoon easy-cook, long grain rice
3 oz (75 g) deep-toned Cheddar cheese, grated
1 oz (25 g) peanuts or walnuts, chopped
1 oz (25 g) mushrooms, chopped
¼ level teaspoon dry mustard
3 tablespoons hot water
To cook
4 tablespoons tomato juice

1. Wash and dry pepper. Cut off top, keep for lid and remove inside fibres and seeds. If necessary, cut a thin sliver off the base of the pepper so that it stands upright without toppling over.
2. Mix together next 6 ingredients. Pack into pepper. Top with lid.
3. Stand in a 1 pint (575 ml) basin. Add tomato juice.
4. Cover with cling wrap. Puncture twice with the tip of a knife to prevent a build-up of steam underneath. (See page 8.)
5. Cook at full power for 6 minutes.
6. Stand 4 minutes. Uncover. Serve.

Tip
Pepper retains a certain appetising crispness.

Watts	Full Power	Defrost
400	8 mins	Nil
500	7 mins	Nil
600	6 mins	Nil
650	5 mins 30 secs	Nil
700	5 mins	Nil

CREAM AVOCADO WITH CROÛTONS

Preparation — fast

With a side dish of salad, this makes a super 'no meat' main course and is an off-beat way of presenting avocado. Quite delicious.

> **1 medium avocado (7 to 8 oz or 200 to 225 g)**
> **½ teaspoon Worcestershire sauce**
> **⅛ level teaspoon salt**
> **3 rounded tablespoons soured cream**
> **1 oz (25 g) mignons morceau (garlic croûtons), broken up into fairly small pieces**

1. Peel avocado. Remove stone. Scoop flesh into a bowl.
2. Lightly beat together the Worcestershire sauce, salt and soured cream. Stir into avocado.
3. Transfer to a 1 pint (575 ml) round dish. Sprinkle with mignons morceau.
4. Cook, uncovered, at full power for 2 minutes.
5. Eat straightaway.

Watts	Full Power	Defrost
400	2 mins 40 secs	Nil
500	2 mins 20 secs	Nil
600	2 mins	Nil
650	1 min 50 secs	Nil
700	1 min 40 secs	Nil

RATATOUILLE

Preparation — a bit time-consuming

The old Mediterranean sunshine charmer, terrific as a copious main course on its own with rice, or served as an accompaniment to omelets, quiches, chicken and burgers. It goes perfectly with lamb chops as well and, if it seems too much for one go, keep half in the fridge up to a week.

6 oz (175 g) aubergine, topped and tailed
4 oz (125 g) green pepper, inside seeds and fibres removed
3 oz (75 g) onions, peeled
6 oz (175 g) tomatoes
4 oz (175 g) courgette or marrow
1 rounded tablespoon tubed or canned tomato purée
1 tablespoon salad oil
⅜ level teaspoon salt
1 heaped tablespoon chopped parsley
1 garlic clove, peeled and crushed

1. Wash and dry first 4 ingredients. Cut all into small dice.
2. Wash courgette and thinly slice. For marrow, peel and cut flesh into small dice.
3. Transfer vegetables to a 2 pint (1 litre) bowl. Stir in purée, oil, salt, parsley and garlic. Mix well.
4. Cover with cling wrap. Puncture twice with the tip of a knife to prevent a build-up of steam underneath. (See page 8.)
5. Cook at full power for 15 minutes.
6. Stand 5 minutes. Uncover. Stir round and serve.

Watts	Full Power	Defrost
400	19 mins 50 secs	Nil
500	17 mins 25 secs	Nil
600	15 mins	Nil
650	13 mins 45 secs	Nil
700	12 mins 35 secs	Nil

MARINATED CAULIFLOWER

Preparation — easy

Crisp and fresh-tasting, this goes extremely well with meat and poultry and is a reliable side dish. Raspberry vinegar and a touch of mint do wonders for the flavour.

6 oz (175 g) cauliflower
⅛ teaspoon salt
2 tablespoons water
1 tablespoon salad oil
2 teaspoons raspberry vinegar
¼ teaspoon bottled mint sauce
½ teaspoon Worcestershire sauce
⅛ level teaspoon salt

1. Break up cauliflower. Sprinkle with salt. Add water.
2. Cover with cling wrap. Puncture twice with the tip of a knife to prevent a build-up of steam underneath. (See page 8.)
3. Cook at full power for 3 minutes.
4. Meanwhile, prepare marinade by beating rest of ingredients together.
5. Uncover cauliflower. Drain. Coat with marinade. Cool.
6. Cover and refrigerate until cold; about 3 to 4 hours.
7. Uncover. Serve.

Watts	Full Power	Defrost
400	4 mins	Nil
500	3 mins 30 secs	Nil
600	3 mins	Nil
650	2 mins 45 secs	Nil
700	2 mins 30 secs	Nil

CAULIFLOWER CREAM CHEESE

Preparation — easy

A variation on cauliflower cheese and still just as tasty whether eaten as a main course or side dish.

7 to 8 oz (200 to 225 g) fresh cauliflower, trimmed weight
¼ level teaspoon salt
3 tablespoons water
1 pack (60 g) St. Ivel cream cheese
1 tablespoon milk
½ level teaspoon prepared mustard (mild or strong, according to taste)

1. Break up cauliflower. Put into dish. Sprinkle with salt. Add water.
2. Cover with cling wrap. Puncture twice with the tip of a knife to prevent a build-up of steam underneath. (See page 8.)
3. Cook at full power for 4 minutes.
4. Leave to stand while preparing sauce.
5. Transfer cheese, milk and mustard to a small dish. Leave uncovered. Melt at defrost setting for 1 minute.
6. Drain cauliflower. Coat with sauce. Leave uncovered. Reheat at full power for 1 minute.

Watts	Full Power	Defrost
400	5 mins 20 secs; 1 min 20 secs	1 min 20 secs
500	4 mins 40 secs; 1 min 10 secs	1 min 10 secs
600	4 mins; 1 min	1 min
650	3 mins 40 secs; 55 secs	55 secs
700	3 mins 20 secs; 50 secs	50 secs

CELERY BRAISE WITH BACON AND CHEESE

Preparation — reasonably quick

A surprise combination of ingredients, resulting in an appetising main course which tastes richer than it is.

6 oz (150 g) fresh celery
½ level teaspoon salt
? tablespoon water
2 oz (50 g) lean, unsmoked gammon
3 tablespoons boiling water
1 level tablespoon finely chopped roasted peanuts, salted or plain

1. Wash and scrub celery clean. Wipe dry. Cut into thin, diagonal slices.
2. Put into a 1 pint (575 ml) round cooking dish. Sprinkle with salt. Add boiling water.
3. Cover with cling wrap. Puncture twice with the tip of a knife to prevent a build-up of steam underneath. (See page 8.) Alternatively, use matching lid.
4. Cook at full power for 7 minutes. Stand 1 minute. Drain.
5. Chop gammon. Stir into celery with cheese. Clean sides of dish with kitchen paper towels.
6. Sprinkle with peanuts. Re-cover as above. Cook at full power for 1 minute. Stand ½ minute. Uncover. Serve.

Watts	Full Power	Defrost
400	9 mins 15 secs; 1 min 20 secs	Nil
500	8 mins 5 secs; 1 min 10 secs	Nil
600	7 mins; 1 min	Nil
650	6 mins 25 secs; 55 secs	Nil
700	5 mins 55 secs; 50 secs	Nil

STUFFED AUBERGINE WITH EGG AND PINE NUTS

Preparation — needs a bit of effort

Whether warm or chilled, this main course vegetable dish is Middle Eastern in character though more delicately flavoured and quite delicious. Accompany with warm pitta bread or Greek bread baked with sesame seeds. You can't go wrong.

1 aubergine weighing 8 to 9 oz (225 to 250 g)
¼ level teaspoon salt
1 tablespoon lemon juice
2 teaspoons salad oil
1 hard boiled egg (page 110), chopped
1 oz (25 g) pine nuts
paprika or chopped parsley for the top

1. Wash and dry aubergine. Prick all over.
2. Put on to a plate. Wrap loosely in one or two kitchen paper towels.
3. Cook at full power for 5 minutes.
4. Stand 2 or 3 minutes. Put on to a board. Cut off green top and throw away.
5. Halve aubergine lengthwise and scoop flesh on to board.
6. Coarsely chop. Tip into bowl. Mix in rest of ingredients (except paprika or parsley).
7. Transfer aubergine shells to a plate. Fill with chopped up mixture and sprinkle with paprika or parsley.
8. Eat straightaway or refrigerate until chilly before serving.

Watts	Full Power	Defrost
400	6 mins 40 secs	Nil
500	5 mins 50 secs	Nil
600	5 mins	Nil
650	4 mins 35 secs	Nil
700	4 mins 10 secs	Nil

BEAN SPROUTS BONANZA

Preparation — effortless

Full of zest, here is a super accompaniment for poultry and some of the more robust fish dishes.

> **4 oz (125 g) bean sprouts**
> **2 lightly rounded tablespoons tomato relish or chutney**
> **½ teaspoon Worcestershire sauce**
> **½ level teaspoon salt**

1. Mix all ingredients together in a 1 pint (575 ml) round cooking dish.
2. Cover with cling wrap. Puncture twice with the tip of a knife to prevent a build-up of steam underneath. (See page 8.)
3. Alternatively, use matching lid.
4. Cook at full power for 3 minutes.
5. Stand 1 minute. Uncover. Stir round and serve.

Watts	Full Power	Defrost
400	4 mins	Nil
500	3 mins 30 secs	Nil
600	3 mins	Nil
650	2 mins 45 secs	Nil
700	2 mins 30 secs	Nil

BUTTERED PUMPKIN WEDGE

Preparation — a doddle

There's more to pumpkin than Cinderella and Halloween and this hefty piece, served sweet or savoury, makes a filling and unusual main course eaten on its own.

1 lb (450 to 500 g) pumpkin, bought as a wedge on a piece of skin

1. Remove seeds, then lay pumpkin on its side on a medium-sized plate.
2. Cover with cling wrap. Puncture twice with the tip of a knife to prevent a build-up of steam underneath. (See page 8.)
3. Cook at full power for 7 minutes.
4. Stand 2 minutes. Uncover. Top with butter or margarine.
5. Serve with a sprinkle of demerara sugar for sweet pumpkin, salt and pepper for savoury. Eat with a spoon.

Watts	Full Power	Defrost
400	9 mins 15 secs	Nil
500	8 mins 5 secs	Nil
600	7 mins	Nil
650	6 mins 25 secs	Nil
700	5 mins 55 secs	Nil

WARM SALAD WITH AVOCADO

Preparation — easy

Highly successful nationwide in top culinary circles, this idea of mine is based on a warm salad I ate at the Fairlawns Hotel in the West Midlands. It was most elegantly presented by Chef Stefan Wilkinson and proved easy to adapt to microwave treatment.

5 teaspoons salad oil
2½ teaspoons vinegar or lemon juice
1 level teaspoon French mustard with peppercorns
½ level teaspoon caster sugar
½ level teaspoon salt
2 medium-sized crisp lettuce leaves
2 radicchio leaves
2 sprays of frisée
½ medium and ripe avocado
8 tortilla chips or mignons morceau (garlic croûtons)

1. Beat together first 5 ingredients to make dressing.
2. Wash lettuce, radicchio and frisée. Drain well. Arrange on a plate.
3. Scoop avocado out of its skin with a teaspoon. Place on top of salad with the tortilla chips or mignons morceau.
4. Coat with dressing. Leave uncovered.
5. Warm through at defrost setting for about ½ minute or until salad feels warm. Serve.

Watts	Full Power	Defrost
400	Nil	40 secs
500	Nil	35 secs
600	Nil	30 secs
650	Nil	28 secs
700	Nil	25 secs

CREAMY MUSHROOMS WITH STILTON

Preparation — quick

A personal pleasure, this rich mushroom dish can be eaten with warm French bread, hot brown toast or boiled potatoes and makes a nutritious and sustaining main course for vegetarians.

4 oz (125 g) button mushrooms
2 oz (50 g) crumbled Stilton cheese
3 tablespoons double cream
½ level teaspoon paprika

1. Wash and dry mushrooms. Put into a 1 pint (575 ml) round dish.
2. Stir in remaining ingredients.
3. Cover with cling wrap. Puncture twice with the tip of a knife to prevent a build-up of steam underneath. (See page 8.)
4. Cook at full power for 2½ minutes. Stand ½ minute.
5. Uncover. Stir round and serve.

Watts	Full Power	Defrost
400	3 mins 20 secs	Nil
500	2 mins 55 secs	Nil
600	2 mins 30 secs	Nil
650	2 mins 20 secs	Nil
700	2 mins 5 secs	Nil

AVOCADO JACKET

Preparation — fairly effortless

Anyone out there interested in healthy eating? If the answer's a resounding yes, you can't go far wrong with a large jacket potato filled with a mildly-seasoned avocado mix. Devoid of animal fat and packed with fibre and vitamins, this makes a super meal for one, the whole thing over and done with in under fifteen minutes.

1 potato weighing 8 oz (or 225 g)
½ medium to large avocado
¼ to ½ level teaspoon salt (or substitute)
¼ level teaspoon onion or garlic salt
¼ level teaspoon paprika
¼ teaspoon Worcestershire sauce

1.   Wash and dry potato. Slash in 2 or 3 places to stop it popping and bursting. Cover with kitchen paper towels.
2.   Cook at full power for 9 minutes. Cloak with a teatowel to keep warm. Stand 5 minutes. Put on to plate.
3.   Scoop avocado flesh into a bowl. Coarsely mash with all remaining ingredients.
4.   Split potato in half. Fill with avocado mixture. Serve.

Watts	Full Power	Defrost
400	11 mins 50 secs	Nil
500	10 mins 25 secs	Nil
600	9 mins	Nil
650	8 mins 15 secs	Nil
700	7 mins 35 secs	Nil

PASTA
AND RICE

All recipes have been tested in a 600 watt oven.
See chart under each for variations of wattage.

BASIC RICE

Preparation — effortless

An easygoing way of cooking rice. It takes only a little less time than conventional cooking but saves fuel and using a saucepan.

3 oz (75 g) easy-cook, long grain rice
¼ level teaspoon salt
½ pt (275 ml) boiling water

1.   Stir all ingredients together in a 1 pint (575 ml) round cooking dish.
2.   Cover with cling wrap. Puncture twice with the tip of a knife to prevent a build-up of steam underneath. (See page 8.) Alternatively, use matching lid.
3.   Cook at full power for 10 minutes.
4.   Stand 5 minutes. Uncover. Drain if necessary. Serve.

Tip
Tasty additions after cooking can include either 1 rounded tablespoon chopped parsley, 1 rounded tablespoon chopped nuts, 4 trimmed and chopped spring onions, a knob of shop-bought herb butter, a chopped hard boiled egg or 2 oz (50 g) shelled prawns. The rice can be re-covered and reheated at full power for 1 minute if it has cooled down too much.

Watts	Full Power	Defrost
400	13 mins 10 secs; 1 min 20 secs (see tip)	Nil
500	11 mins 35 secs; 1 min 10 secs (see tip)	Nil
600	10 mins; 1 min (see tip)	Nil
650	9 mins 10 secs; 55 secs (see tip)	Nil
700	8 mins 25 secs; 50 secs (see tip)	Nil

HOT RICE SALAD

Preparation — a tiny bit demanding

A bright and crisp contribution is this off-beat hot salad geared for vegetarians, speckled with cucumber, tomato and sunflower seeds. Try it with brown rolls.

3 oz (75 g) easy-cook, long grain rice
½ level teaspoon salt
½ pt (275 ml) boiling water
1 carton (3½ oz or 100 g) fromage frais
2 level tablespoons sunflower seeds
2 oz (50 g) unpeeled and washed cucumber
3 oz (75 g) tomatoes, washed and dried
extra salt and pepper to taste

1. Put rice, salt and water into a 1 pint (575 ml) round cooking dish.
2. Cover with cling wrap. Puncture twice with the tip of a knife to prevent a build-up of steam underneath. (See page 8.) Alternatively, use matching lid.
3. Cook at full power for 10 minutes. Stand 5 minutes. Uncover. Drain if necessary.
4. Mix in fromage frais and sunflower seeds.
5. Coarsely chop cucumber and tomatoes. Fork into rice. Season to taste.
6. Re-cover with a lid, plate or saucer. Cook at full power for 2½ minutes. Stand 1 minute. Uncover. Stir round and serve.

Watts	Full Power	Defrost
400	13 mins 10 secs; 3 mins 20 secs	Nil
500	11 mins 35 secs; 2 mins 55 secs	Nil
600	10 mins; 2 mins 30 secs	Nil
650	9 mins 10 secs; 2 mins 20 secs	Nil
700	8 mins 25 secs; 2 mins 5 secs	Nil

CHEESEY RICE

Preparation — easy

An appetising little meal which is complete in itself, though a salad or dish of seasonal vegetables suits well.

3 oz (75 g) easy-cook, long grain rice
¼ level teaspoon salt
½ pt (275 ml) boiling water
2 oz (50 g) red Leicester cheese, grated
2 tablespoons milk
½ to 1 level teaspoon mild mustard
1 level tablespoon packeted wholemeal breadcrumbs

1. Put rice, salt and water into a 1 pint (575 ml) round cooking dish.
2. Cover with cling wrap. Puncture twice with the tip of a knife to prevent a build-up of steam underneath. (See page 8.) Alternatively, use matching lid.
3. Cook at full power for 10 minutes. Stand 5 minutes. Uncover. Drain if necessary.
4. Stir in cheese, milk and mustard. Tidy up dish round edges.
5. Sprinkle top of rice with crumbs. Leave uncovered. Reheat at full power for 1 minute. Stand ½ minute. Serve.

Watts	Full Power	Defrost
400	13 mins 10 secs. 1 min 20 secs	Nil
500	11 mins 35 secs; 1 min 10 secs	Nil
600	10 mins; 1 min	Nil
650	9 mins 10 secs; 55 secs	Nil
700	8 mins 25 secs; 50 secs	Nil

SHORT-CUT VEGETABLE RISOTTO

Preparation — effortless

It takes seconds to put together and ends up as a flavoursome risotto which, with grated cheese, may be eaten as a dish on its own. Left plain, it can accompany poultry, fish, cheese, egg and some meat dishes, especially veal.

3 oz (75 g) easy-cook, long grain rice
½ level teaspoon salt
½ pt (275 ml) boiling water
1 level tablespoon mixed dried peppers
1 level tablespoon dried sliced mushrooms
1 level tablespoon dried celery

1. Stir all ingredients together in a 1 pint (575 ml) round cooking dish.
2. Cover with cling wrap. Puncture twice with the tip of a knife to prevent a build-up of steam underneath. (See page 8.) Alternatively, use matching lid.
3. Cook at full power for 10 minutes. Stand 5 minutes.
4. Uncover. Stir round and serve.

Watts	Full Power	Defrost
400	13 mins 10 secs	Nil
500	11 mins 35 secs	Nil
600	10 mins	Nil
650	9 mins 10 secs	Nil
700	8 mins 25 secs	Nil

PLAIN PASTA

Preparation — almost effortless

Cooked in the dish in which it's to be served, this saves using a saucepan and washing-up. Additionally, the pasta keeps its shape and remains slightly firm to the bite.

2 oz (50 g) pasta such as spaghetti, macaroni, shells, twists, etc.
¼ level teaspoon salt
8 fluid oz (225 ml) boiling water

1. Put pasta into a 1 pint (575 ml) bowl, breaking up spaghetti into shortish lengths.
2. Add salt and water.
3. Leave uncovered. Cook at full power for 7 minutes.
4. Remove from microwave. Cover with a plate or saucer. Stand 3 minutes.
5. Uncover. Stir round again. Serve.

Watts	Full Power	Defrost
400	9 mins 15 secs	Nil
500	8 mins 5 secs	Nil
600	7 mins	Nil
650	6 mins 25 secs	Nil
700	5 mins 55 secs	Nil

PASTA CREMA

Preparation — requires a bit of effort

Want to pamper yourself? Try this glitzy meal, full of riches and calories.

> **3 oz (75 g) fresh pasta such as flat noodles or spirals**
> **½ pt (275 ml) boiling water**
> **½ level teaspoon salt**
> **2 oz (50 g) lean ham, chopped**
> **2 level tablespoons chopped parsley**
> **2 slightly rounded tablespoons soured or double cream**
> **2 tablespoons tomato juice**

1. Put pasta, water and salt into a 1¾ pint (1 litre) bowl
2. Cover with cling wrap. Puncture twice with the tip of a knife to prevent a build-up of steam underneath. (See page 8.)
3. Cook at full power for 5 minutes. Stand 1 minute.
4. Drain. Leave pasta in bowl. Add remaining ingredients.
5. Toss well to mix. Re-cover as above.
6. Cook at full power for 1½ minutes.
7. Stand 1 minute. Uncover. Stir round and serve.

Watts	Full Power	Defrost
400	6 mins 40 secs; 2 mins	Nil
500	5 mins 50 secs; 1 min 45 secs	Nil
600	5 mins; 1 min 30 secs	Nil
650	4 mins 35 secs; 1 min 25 secs	Nil
700	4 mins 10 secs; 1 min 15 secs	Nil

PLAIN FRESH PASTA

Cook as Pasta Crema. Cook, stand, drain. Toss with a little butter or margarine. Alternatively, serve with any sauce to taste.

TORTELLONI IN CLEAR SOUP

Preparation — a doddle

What better than fresh tortelloni in the simplest of soups, very much in the style of classic Italian cooking? It makes a warming starter or even a sustaining main course with a bowl of salad and a brown roll for company.

> **3 oz (75 g) fresh tortelloni with ricotta cheese filling (about 11 pieces)**
> **½ pt (275 ml) boiling water**
> **1 chicken, beef or vegetable stock cube**

1. Put tortelloni into a roomy soup bowl.
2. Add water. Crumble in cube.
3. Cover with cling wrap. Puncture twice with the tip of a knife to prevent a build-up of steam underneath. (See page 8.)
4. Cook at full power for 5 minutes.
5. Stand 1 minute. Uncover. Stir round and serve.

Watts	Full Power	Defrost
400	6 mins 40 secs	Nil
500	5 mins 50 secs	Nil
600	5 mins	Nil
650	4 mins 35 secs	Nil
700	4 mins 10 secs	Nil

DESSERTS

All recipes have been tested in a 600 watt oven.
See chart under each for variations of wattage.

STEWED APRICOTS

Preparation — needs a bit of your time

With all the cans of fruit around, stewed fruit is becoming a forgotten art which I urge you to revive with the help of your microwave. The taste and colour of the fruit is superb, whether eaten by itself or with custard, and a one-portion amount is ready in about five minutes flat.

> **6 fresh apricots (4 oz or 125 g)**
> **1½ level tablespoons granulated sugar**
> **2 tablespoons water**

1. Well wash apricots. Halve and remove stones.
2. Put fruit into serving bowl.
3. Stir in sugar and water.
4. Cover with cling wrap. Puncture twice with the tip of a knife to prevent a build-up of steam underneath. (See page 8.)
5. Cook at defrost setting for 5 minutes.
6. Stand 1 minute. Uncover. Eat hot or cold.

STEWED APPLES

Make exactly as stewed apricots, using 8 oz (225 g) trimmed weight of peeled, cored and sliced apples. Increase sugar to 2½ level tablespoons and water to 1½ tablespoons. Add a clove. Cook as below, allowing a few seconds extra if apples are too firm for personal taste.

Watts	Full Power	Defrost
400	Nil	6 mins 40 secs
500	Nil	5 mins 50 secs
600	Nil	5 mins
650	Nil	4 mins 35 secs
700	Nil	4 mins 10 secs

STEWED RHUBARB

Make exactly as stewed apples using 4 oz (125 g) rhubarb, trimmed weight, cut up into small pieces. Increase sugar to 2½ level tablespoons.

HOT FRUIT FOAM

Preparation — requires a bit of effort

Looks like a mountain of foam and makes a generous pud for one. It is light and airy, not too sweet and partners well with ginger snaps or sponge fingers. For a note of cheer, the foam can be topped with a dollop of red jam or sprinkling of crunchy demerara sugar.

1 can (128 g) Heinz baby food, consisting of pure fruit purée (apple and pear) with no added sugar
1 grade 2 egg, separated
pinch of salt

1. Tip fruit purée into a bowl.
2. Stir in egg yolk thoroughly.
3. Beat egg white stiffly with pinch of salt. Fold gently and smoothly into fruit mixture.
4. Transfer to very lightly greased 1 pint (575 ml) basin. Cook, uncovered, at full power for 1½ minutes.

Watts	Full Power	Defrost
400	2 mins	Nil
500	1 min 45 secs	Nil
600	1 min 30 secs	Nil
650	1 min 25 secs	Nil
700	1 min 15 secs	Nil

LEMON BAKED APPLE

Preparation — a little demanding

As fresh as an orchard in spring, why not treat yourself to this tangy baked apple, packed with lemon curd and simmered in apple juice? Or its close friend, filled with brown sugar and dates and cocooned in honey? Both are meals in themselves and put the finishing touch to a fast snack such as a sandwich, filled croissant or something on toast.

1 Bramley apple (12 oz or 350 g)
7 teaspoons lemon curd
9 chocolate dots
3 tablespoons apple juice

1. Wash and dry apple. Score a line round the apple with a sharp knife, about one-third of the way down from the top.
2. Remove core with a potato peeler, taking care not to cut through the base or filling will seep out.
3. Fill with curd. Top with chocolate dots. Transfer to bowl. Pour in apple juice.
4. Cover with cling wrap. Puncture twice with the tip of a knife to prevent a build-up of steam underneath. (See page 8.)
5. Cook at defrost setting for 10 minutes when apple should puff up like a soufflé.
6. Stand 2 minutes. Uncover. Serve.

DATE AND HONEY BAKED APPLE

Make exactly as above, filling the centre with 1½ oz (4 oz) chopped dates and 1 level tablespoon demerara sugar. Put into dish and surround with honey.

Watts	Full Power	Defrost
400	Nil	13 mins 10 secs
500	Nil	11 mins 35 secs
600	Nil	10 mins
650	Nil	9 mins 10 secs
700	Nil	8 mins 25 secs

LALINE'S KISS

Preparation — easy

Culled from one of London's newest and smartest French Brasseries called Laline, you must try this glamorous and highly sophisticated sweet. Don't let the pepper startle you — it is the perfect way of bringing out the full taste of the fruit.

| ½ oz (15 g) butter |
| 4 oz (125 g) strawberries |
| ½ level teaspoon coarsely crushed black peppercorns |

1. Put butter into a serving dish.
2. Melt at defrost setting for about 1 minute.
3. Wash, hull and halve strawberries lengthwise.
4. Add to butter with pepper. Toss to mix.
5. Cover with a saucer or plate.
6. Cook at defrost setting for 1¼ minutes.
7. Top with a scoop of vanilla ice cream.

Watts	Full Power	Defrost
400	Nil	1 min 20 secs; 1 min 35 secs
500	Nil	1 min 10 secs; 1 min 25 secs
600	Nil	1 min; 1 min 15 secs
650	Nil	55 secs; 1 min 10 secs
700	Nil	50 secs; 1 min 5 secs

GROUND RICE PUDDING

Preparation — attention-seeking

I'm not going to say that making milk pudding in the microwave is any easier than on top of the hob in a saucepan, but it rarely sticks, can't burn and never lumps. All plus points.

> **1 level tablespoon ground rice**
> **2 level teaspoons caster sugar**
> **¼ pt (150 ml) milk**
> **cinnamon or mixed spice**

1.   Put rice and sugar into a 2½ pint (1.5 litre) basin as it needs room to rise.
2.   Work in milk smoothly. Add a plastic spoon to basin for stirring.
3.   Leave uncovered. Cook at full power for 1½ minutes. Stir well. Continue to cook a further 1½ minutes, stirring at the end of every ½ minute.
4.   Stand 1 minute. Sprinkle with cinnamon or mixed spice. Serve.

SEMOLINA PUDDING

Make exactly as Ground Rice Pudding, substituting fine semolina for rice.

Watts	Full Power	Defrost
400	4 mins	Nil
500	3 mins 30 secs	Nil
600	3 mins	Nil
650	2 mins 45 secs	Nil
700	2 mins 30 secs	Nil

CUSTARD

Make exactly as Ground Rice Pudding but cook for 2½ minutes only and stir at the end of every ½ minute.

Watts	Full Power	Defrost
400	3 mins 20 secs	Nil
500	2 mins 55 secs	Nil
600	2 mins 30 secs	Nil
650	2 mins 20 secs	Nil
700	2 mins 5 secs	Nil

FRUITED BUN PUDDING IN EGG CUSTARD

Preparation — easy

A stunner. And generously proportioned.

2 fruited tea buns
¼ pt (150 ml) milk
1 oz (25 g) butter or margarine
1 Grade 2 egg
1 rounded tablespoon demerara sugar

1. Halve buns. Leave on one side temporarily.
2. Pour milk into a jug or bowl. Add butter or margarine. Heat, uncovered, until fat melts for 1¼ minutes at full power. Beat in egg.
3. Put buns, cut sides up, into a 6 inch (15 cm) square dish.
4. Coat with milk mixture. Sprinkle with sugar.
5. Leave uncovered. Cook at defrost setting for 8 minutes.
6. Stand 2 minutes. Serve.

Watts	Full Power	Defrost
400	1 min 35 secs	10 mins 30 secs
500	1 min 25 secs	9 mins 15 secs
600	1 min 15 secs	8 mins
650	1 min 10 secs	7 mins 20 secs
700	1 min 5 secs	6 mins 45 secs

BABY BUN PUDDING

Use 1 halved bun but keep rest of ingredients the same. Put into a 1 pint (575 ml) round dish and follow directions above. Leave uncovered and cook at defrost setting for 8 minutes.

Watts	Full Power	Defrost
400	1 min 35 secs	10 mins 30 secs
500	1 min 25 secs	9 mins 15 secs
600	1 min 15 secs	8 mins
650	1 min 10 secs	7 mins 20 secs
700	1 mins 5 secs	6 mins 45 secs

BAKED EGG CUSTARD

Preparation — simple

Always popular, nothing could be easier to make than this single serving traditional custard, the flavour enhanced with vanilla and nutmeg. Eat warm or cold and either leave plain or accompany with seasonal fresh or stewed fruit — canned if it's easier.

1 Grade 2 egg

4 tablespoons milk

2 level teaspoons caster sugar

3 drops vanilla essence

½ level teaspoon cornflour

½ level teaspoon nutmeg

1. Beat all ingredients well together in a small basin.
2. Pour into a dessert dish. Leave uncovered.
3. Cook at defrost setting for 4¾ minutes.
4. Leave until warm or cold. Serve as desired with fruit, cream, ice cream.

Watts	Full Power	Defrost
400	Nil	6 mins 15 secs
500	Nil	5 mins 30 secs
600	Nil	4 mins 45 secs
650	Nil	4 mins 25 secs
700	Nil	4 mins

JAM SPONGE PUDDING

Preparation — easy

Moist, tender and light — a lovely pudding to make for oneself and enjoy with a cup of coffee at the end of a meal.

2 oz (50 g) self-raising flour
1 oz 625 g) caster sugar
1 oz (25 g) butter or margarine
1 Grade 2 egg, beaten
2 tablespoons milk
¼ teaspoon vanilla essence
2 level tablespoons bright red jam

1. Sift flour into a bowl. Toss in sugar.
2. Rub in butter or margarine finely.
3. Using a fork, mix to a soft consistency with next 3 ingredients. Leave aside for the moment.
4. Spoon jam into a greased 1 pint (575 ml) basin. Leave uncovered.
5. Heat at full power for ½ minute. Add pudding mixture.
6. Cover with cling wrap. Puncture twice with the tip of a knife to prevent a build-up of steam underneath. (See page 8.)
7. Cook at full power for 1½ minutes. Stand 1 minute.
8. Uncover. Turn out of basin. Serve.

Watts	Full Power	Defrost
400	40 secs; 2 mins	Nil
500	35 secs; 1 min 45 secs	Nil
600	30 secs; 1 min 30 secs	Nil
650	28 secs; 1 min 25 secs	Nil
700	25 secs; 1 min 15 secs	Nil

RAISIN SPONGE PUDDING

Preparation — easy

Good and homely, especially with hot custard swished over the top.

2 oz (50 g) self-raising flour
1 oz (25 g) caster sugar
1 oz (25 g) butter or margarine
1 oz (25 g) raisins
1 Grade 2 egg, beaten
2 tablespoons milk

1. Sift flour into a bowl. Toss in sugar.
2. Rub in butter or margarine finely. Add raisins.
3. Using a fork, mix to a soft consistency with last 2 ingredients.
4. Spoon into a greased, 1 pint (575 ml) basin.
5. Cover with cling wrap. Puncture twice with the tip of a knife to prevent a build-up of steam underneath. (See page 8.)
6. Cook at full power for 1½ minutes. Stand 1 minute.
7. Cook a further ½ minute. Uncover. Turn out of basin. Serve.

Tip
Currants or sultanas may be used instead of raisins

Watts	Full Power	Defrost
400	2 mins; 40 secs	Nil
500	1 min 45 secs; 35 secs	Nil
600	1 min 30 secs; 30 secs	Nil
650	1 min 25 secs; 20 secs	Nil
700	1 min 15 secs; 25 secs	Nil

MAPLE AND PECAN PUDDING

Preparation — requires some attention

Bathed in maple syrup, this is based on a Canadian recipe with a stunning flavour. Try it with whipped cream or a generous topping of spooning cream.

> **2 oz (50 g) 100% wholemeal self-raising flour**
> **1 oz (25 g) light brown soft sugar**
> **1 oz (25 g) butter or margarine**
> **1 oz (25 g) pecan nuts or walnuts, coarsely chopped**
> **1 Grade 2 egg, beaten**
> **2 tablespoons milk**
> **2 tablespoons maple syrup**

1. Tip flour into a bowl. Toss in sugar.
2. Rub in butter or margarine finely. Add nuts.
3. Using a fork, mix to a soft consistency with next 2 ingredients. Leave aside for the moment.
4. Spoon syrup into a greased 1 pint (575 ml) basin. Leave uncovered.
5. Heat at full power for ½ minute. Add pudding mixture.
6. Cover with cling wrap. Puncture twice with the tip of a knife to prevent a build-up of steam underneath. (See page 8.)
7. Cook at full power for 2 minutes. Stand 1 minute.
8. Uncover. Turn out of basin. Serve.

Watts	Full Power	Defrost
400	40 secs; 2 mins 40 secs	Nil
500	35 secs; 2 mins 20 secs	Nil
600	30 secs; 2 mins	Nil
650	28 secs; 1 min 50 secs	Nil
700	25 secs; 1 min 40 secs	Nil

CHOCOLATE PUDDING

Preparation — requires some attention

One of the most popular puddings of all, this microwave version is top gear stuff and is ready in 3 minutes. Serve with cream, custard or chocolate ice cream.

1½ oz (40 g) self-raising flour
½ oz (15 g) cocoa powder
1 oz (25 g) light brown soft sugar
1 oz (25 g) butter or margarine
1 Grade 2 egg, beaten
3 tablespoons milk
¼ teaspoon vanilla essence

1. Sift flour and cocoa into a bowl. Toss in sugar.
2. Rub in butter or margarine finely.
3. Using a fork, mix to a soft consistency with last 3 ingredients.
4. Spoon into a greased, 1 pint (575 ml) basin.
5. Cover with cling wrap. Puncture twice with the tip of a knife to prevent a build-up of steam underneath. (See page 8.)
6. Cook at full power for 1½ minutes. Stand 1 minute.
7. Cook a further ½ minute. Uncover. Turn out of basin. Serve.

Watts	Full Power	Defrost
400	2 mins; 40 secs	Nil
500	1 min 45 secs; 35 secs	Nil
600	1 min 30 secs; 30 secs	Nil
650	1 min 25 secs; 28 secs	Nil
700	1 min 15 secs; 25 secs	Nil

SYRUP SUET PUDDING

Preparation — fast

A delicious, spongy pudding for winter which 'steams' to a turn in 2 minutes.

2 level tablespoons golden syrup
2 oz (50 g) self-raising flour
1 oz (25 g) beef or vegetable suet (I favour the latter)
1 oz (25 g) caster sugar
1 Grade 2 egg, beaten
2 tablespoons milk

1. Put syrup into base of a 1 pint (575 ml) greased basin.
2. Leave uncovered. Heat at full power for ½ minute.
3. Tip flour, suet and sugar into a bowl. Toss over and over with fingertips.
4. Using a fork, mix to a soft consistency with egg and milk.
5. Spoon into basin over hot syrup.
6. Cover with cling wrap. Puncture twice with the tip of a knife to prevent a build-up of steam underneath. (See page 8.)
7. Cook at full power for 1½ minutes. Stand 1 minute.
8. Uncover. Turn out of basin. Serve with custard, cream or nothing.

Watts	Full Power	Defrost
400	40 secs; 2 mins	Nil
500	35 secs; 1 min 45 secs	Nil
600	30 secs; 1 min 30 secs	Nil
650	28 secs; 1 min 25 secs	Nil
700	25 secs; 1 min 15 secs	Nil

A SORT OF SPOTTED DICK

Preparation — fast

A tried and trusted friend, this works like a charm and, with a dollop of cream, custard or syrup, brings back fond memories of happy childhood puds.

2 oz (50 g) self-raising flour
1 oz (25 g) beef or vegetable suet (I favour the latter)
1 oz (25 g) caster sugar
1 oz (25 g) raisins or sultanas (or mixture of both)
1 Grade 2 egg, beaten
2 tablespoons milk

1. Tip first 4 ingredients into a bowl.
2. Using a fork, mix to a soft consistency with egg and milk.
3. Spoon into a greased 1 pint (575 ml) basin.
4. Cover with cling wrap. Puncture twice with the tip of a knife to prevent a build-up of steam underneath. (See page 8.)
5. Cook at full power for 2 minutes. Stand 1 minute.
6. Cook a further ½ minute. Uncover. Turn out of basin. Serve.

Watts	Full Power	Defrost
400	2 mins 40 secs; 40 secs	Nil
500	2 mins 20 secs; 35 secs	Nil
600	2 mins; 30 secs	Nil
650	1 min 50 secs; 28 secs	Nil
700	1 min 40 secs; 25 secs	Nil

APPLE AND ORANGE BUBBLES

Preparation — quite easy and fairly fast — but needs a bit of attention

Cool, light, economical and a beautiful spring or early summer sweet.

4 cubes orange jelly (¼ of a packet)
cold water
5 oz (150 g) apple purée, canned or homemade
1 Grade 2 egg
pinch of salt

1. Separate jelly into 4 individual cubes by cutting with kitchen scissors.
2. Put into measuring jug. Make up to 3 fluid ounces (75 ml) with cold water. Leave uncovered.
3. Heat at defrost setting for 2½ minutes.
4. Stir until jelly is absolutely clear. Stir in apple purée and egg yolk.
5. Refrigerate until just beginning to thicken and set.
6. Beat egg white and salt together until stiff and peaky.
7. Lightly fold into apple mixture with a metal spoon.
8. Transfer to a serving bowl. Refrigerate at least 4 hours before eating.

Tip
If liked, decorate to taste before serving with hundreds and thousands, chocolate strands, fresh mint leaves, chopped nuts etc. Also, other kinds of fruit purée may be used in place of apple.

Watts	Full Power	Defrost
400	Nil	3 mins 20 secs
500	Nil	2 mins 55 secs
600	Nil	2 mins 30 secs
650	Nil	2 mins 30 secs
700	Nil	2 mins 5 secs

TREAT TIME MINT CHOC MOUSSE

Preparation — speedy and worth every second

A delicious, albeit calorie-laden, mousse with a hint of mint which is made from a bar of peppermint cream and one egg. You can't go wrong but eat within four hours as mousse separates out if it's left to stand for too long.

> **1 bar (200 g) Fry's peppermint cream, at room temperature**
> **1 Grade 2 egg, at room temperature**
> **pinch of salt**

1. Break up chocolate cream and put into a basin.
2. Melt, uncovered, at defrost setting for 1½ minutes.
3. Separate egg. Stir yolk into chocolate.
4. Beat egg white and pinch of salt to a stiff snow.
5. Fold into chocolate mixture. Spoon into dessert dish.
6. Cover with saucer or small plate. Refrigerate at least 1 hour before eating.

CHOCOLATE CREAM MOUSSE

Make exactly as above, using a 200 g bar of Fry's chocolate cream.

Watts	Full Power	Defrost
400	Nil	2 mins
500	Nil	1 min 45 secs
600	Nil	1 min 30 secs
650	Nil	1 min 25 secs
700	Nil	1 min 15 secs

PERFECTLY NATURAL CHRISTMAS PUDDING

Preparation — effortless

A little gem, not too rich, and a neat one-person serving with either traditional brandy butter, whipped cream or custard. And the major plus is that the pudding cooks in a amazing two and a half minutes flat. Also it's made with natural ingredients to include vegetable suet.

½ oz (15 g) 100% self-raising wholemeal flour
½ oz (15 g) fresh brown breadcrumbs
½ oz (15 g) vegetable suet
1 oz (25 g) dark brown molasses sugar
1 level teaspoon mixed spice
4 oz (125 g) mixed dried fruit
1 Grade 2 egg beaten lightly
1 tablespoon liquid coffee-essence such as Camp

1. Tip first 6 ingredients into a bowl. Toss over and over with fingertips.
2. Using a fork, mix to a soft consistency with egg and coffee essence.
3. Transfer to a 1 pint (575 ml) lightly greased basin.
4. Cover with cling wrap. Puncture twice with the tip of a knife to prevent a build-up of steam underneath. (See page 8.)
5. Cook at full power for 1 minute. Stand 1 minute. Cook a further ½ minute at full power.
6. Stand ½ minute. Uncover. Turn out on to a plate. Serve.

Watts	Full Power	Defrost
400	2 mins	Nil
500	1 mins 45 secs	Nil
600	1 mins 30 secs	Nil
650	1 mins 25 secs	Nil
700	1 mins 15 secs	Nil

HONEYPOT BANANAS WITH RUM

Preparation — fast and easy

A warm pleasure to come home to on a chilly day. The banana is enough on its own but may be embellished with cream or ice cream.

| 1 medium banana (4 oz or 125 g) |
| 1 tablespoon clear honey |
| 2 teaspoons rum |
| 1 level teaspoon demerara sugar |

1. Peel and slice banana. Put into a dessert dish.
2. Coat with honey or rum. Sprinkle with sugar. Leave uncovered.
3. Heat at defrost setting for 1 minute. Serve.

Watts	Full Power	Defrost
400	Nil	1 min 20 secs
500	Nil	1 min 10 secs
600	Nil	1 min
650	Nil	55 secs
700	Nil	50 secs

SHERRY ORANGE

Preparation — easy

A refreshing sweet for anytime.

1 large orange
2 level tablespoons demerara sugar
3 tablespoons sherry

1.   Peel orange, removing all traces of white pith.
2.   Cut into fairly thin slices. Put into a dessert dish.
3.   Put sugar and sherry into a small dish. Leave uncovered.
4.   Heat at defrost setting for 3 minutes.
5.   Stir briskly until liquid is clear. Spoon over oranges.
6.   Refrigerate 4 to 5 hours before serving.

Watts	Full Power	Defrost
400	Nil	4 mins
500	Nil	3 mins 30 secs
600	Nil	3 mins
650	Nil	2 mins 45 secs
700	Nil	2 mins 30 secs

JELLIED SUNSHINE

Preparation — child's play

A fresh-tasting, golden yellow dessert based on jelly and fresh mango. It's something of a luxury but worth making once in a while when you've something to sing about.

4 cubes lemon jelly (¼ of a packet)
cold water
1 small mango weighing about 8 oz or 225 g

1. Separate jelly into 4 individual cubes by cutting with kitchen scissors.
2. Put into measuring jug. Make up to ¼ pt (150 ml) with cold water. Leave uncovered.
3. Heat at defrost setting for 3 minutes.
4. Stir until jelly is absolutely clear. Cool and refrigerate until just beginning to thicken and set.
5. Cut mango into small dice. Put into dessert dish. Coat with jelly. Set in the refrigerator.

Watts	Full Power	Defrost
400	Nil	4 mins
500	Nil	3 mins 30 secs
600	Nil	3 mins
650	Nil	2 mins 45 secs
700	Nil	2 mins 30 secs

FIGS MARINADED IN LIME TEA

Preparation — fairly easy

If anyone likes an interesting dessert, this is it. It's also extremely palatable for breakfast on a hot summer's day, refrigerator cold and eaten with muesli.

1 tea bag
¼ pt (150 ml) cold water
2 level teaspoons caster sugar
2 tablespoons lime cordial
6 ready-to-eat dried figs

1. Put tea bag into a cup or jug. Add water.
2. Leave uncovered. Heat at full power for 1¾ minutes.
3. Strain into a serving bowl.
4. Add lime cordial and figs.
5. Cover. Leave to stand overnight.

Watts	Full Power	Defrost
400	2 mins 25 secs	Nil
500	2 mins 5 secs	Nil
600	1 min 45 secs	Nil
650	1 min 35 secs	Nil
700	1 min 25 secs	Nil

INDEX